# GARRETT ECKBO

Taub garden. Los Angeles,
1957.

[Documents Collection]

For Arline Williams Eckbo

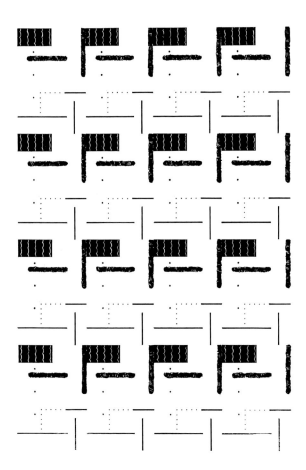

Exterior space and
enclosure study.
Unidentified project.
Site plan.
Circa 1950.
[Documents Collection]

For Arline Williams Eckbo

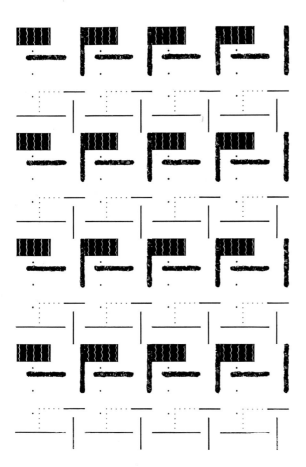

Exterior space and
enclosure study.
Unidentified project.
Site plan.
Circa 1950.
[*Documents Collection*]

## PREFACE

Through over fifty years of practice, writing, and teaching, Garrett Eckbo has been one of the most influential landscape architects of this century, fitting design to the needs and desires of contemporary life. His contribution is distinct for addressing in equal measure society, the natural landscape, art, and technique. While so many modern American landscape architects focused on the private garden — and later the corporate landscape — Eckbo designed also in the public sphere, at times, for the lowest stratum of society. For him, landscape design was also an art, but a social art.

This book accompanies the exhibition *Garrett Eckbo: Modern Landscapes for Living*, which opens at the University Art Museum in Berkeley in January 1997. It is neither a catalog for the exhibition nor a definitive biography of the landscape architect (an impossible task given stringent time restrictions). Our simple intention has been to reintroduce ideas and landscapes by Garrett Eckbo to a new professional and general audience, examining the social, artistic, and professional contexts in which his work was situated.

The first essay outlines the events in Eckbo's life and the course of his development as a landscape architect. His vision of landscape design differed from many contemporaries in its philosophical grounding in the social as well as artistic matrices of the era. In the late 1930s, having barely completed his graduate studies, he coauthored a series of articles (with James Rose and Dan Kiley) calling for a comprehensive view of landscape design that acknowledged the interrelated realms of the primeval (wilderness), rural, and urban (developed) environments. His aesthetic contributions first centered in the urban or suburban arenas — particularly regarding community and residential landscape design — and in later years his practice executed an increased number of commissions for broad-scale planning and ecological management. Such active involvement with greater environmental issues led to his firm's preparation of studies as diverse as the open-space master plan for all of California and a management plan for Niagara Falls.

In part the constraints of time and space, in part the diffuse responsibility for large collaborative projects, have caused us to center our inquiry on the years 1935 through 1955, to focus on design proper, rather than landscape study and management. This decision resulted also from expedience. Since the College of Environmental Design Documents Collection at the University of California at Berkeley now holds most of the Eckbo papers from the early years, it became our source for all graphic materials other than photographs. The compressed schedule for producing the exhibition and book — under a year — demanded such pragmatic considerations.

The period under inquiry covers Eckbo's education and emergence as an internationally recognized professional, one segment of a career that would extend over three additional decades. Eckbo's writings, for example, warrant more discussion than presented here; his role as an educator at the University of Southern California and his alma mater, the University of California at Berkeley, require further examination. Certainly, more research and study are needed, not only to set out the full range of Garrett Eckbo's accomplishment, but also to understand a significant part of the profession and discipline of landscape architecture in the twentieth century.

Within our chronological span of 1935 through 1955 — between Eckbo's university education and the expansion of his office into fully corporate practice — we try to outline the broad scope of his ideas and designs at any given moment. Unusually, even in his student years at Harvard (1936-38), Eckbo's vision — prompted by the social vision of Walter Gropius, who headed architectural studies there — always transcended the individual house and garden. A neighborhood, a community, symbolized the American democracy, balancing the will of the individual with that of the collective body. While an individual expressed personal freedom in the garden — and Eckbo helped realize that expression — he or she bore a responsibility toward the community as a body and toward all natural systems as a whole. Eckbo's ideas remain equally poignant today, his proclamations equally viable.

A number of people have contributed significantly to our work. First, we need to thank Garrett Eckbo himself for providing memories and information, drawings, photographs, and considerable amounts of good cheer — and for composing a suitable afterword.

To Arline Williams Eckbo, our thanks for her encouragement, hospitality, collective memory, numerous clarifications where documentation failed, insights, vignettes — and her presence in Garrett's life all these years. He is, no doubt, a better person for it.

We also thank Michael Laurie, Reuben Rainey, and Robert Riley for their continued support and critical reading of earlier versions of our manuscript. Lisa Howard provided valuable research assistance. At the Documents Collection, Paul Burgin was ever-pleasant, always willing to locate materials and arrange their photography; Stephen Tobriner helped make the drawings available for both the exhibition and the book. University Art Museum curator of collections, James Steward, with the museum director, Jacquelyn Baas, shared our enthusiasm for the project from the very start and did everything possible to make the path toward its realization a smooth one. Nina Zurier also warrants our thanks for her professional design expertise and consultation on mounting the exhibition. We warmly appreciate all their efforts.

The stunning photographs by Julius Shulman were a critical addition to the record and beauty of both the exhibition and this publication. He graciously shared his images and an afternoon of his time, providing drinks and tasty pastry, facts and anecdotes, and a wealth of documentation on architecture and landscape architecture in California. To him, and to the other lenders, we offer our gratitude.

With the University of California Press we have had a nearly ideal collaboration. Valeurie Friedman and Sheila Levine saw the merit in the project and swiftly dealt with all potential problems with efficiency and good humor. Edith Gladstone whipped the manuscript into shape under very tight deadlines, keeping our linguistic color while rendering it, if not grammatically perfect, at least grammatically acceptable. Jenny Tomlin undertook the proofreading. At the production end, Mark Schwettmann aided enormously in preparing and honing the electronic versions of the design; Sam Rosenthal at the University of California Press saw the project through printing. We offer our thanks to one and all.

Although his efforts were not ready for photography at the time of publication, and thus could not be used as illustrations for this book, we want to thank Jason Brody for producing for the exhibition some fine models of a selection of Eckbo projects. Similarly, there are bound to be friends and colleagues who will help realize the exhibition long after the book has gone to press. Let us here offer our apologies for not mentioning them by name; the gratitude is there nonetheless.

A note: dating gardens is a rather slippery process that eludes precision. When is a garden ever done? When should one assign a date: at the time of design, the time of completion, or when the vegetation has matured? What if only a part of the garden was constructed by a certain date? We settle on the date of occupancy, a reasonable practice common in architectural history, as the date assigned the landscape design. For unrealized projects we use the date of design. We acknowledge, however, that this process is less than perfect and is certainly open to challenge.

And a final note: all designs are principally by Garrett Eckbo, unless otherwise noted. All sites mentioned are in California, unless otherwise qualified.

Marc Treib
Dorothée Imbert

Berkeley
June 1996

Taft Defense Housing.
San Joaquin Valley,
1941. Farm Security
Administration.

[*Documents Collection*]

# GARRETT
# ECKBO

## MODERN
## LANDSCAPES
## FOR LIVING

# THE SOCIAL ART OF LANDSCAPE DESIGN

## Marc Treib

In the title of his first major publication, Garrett Eckbo encapsulated his definition of, and attitude toward, landscape design. *Landscape for Living* rejected the garden and the park as provider of mere visual pleasure, as the setting for horticultural display alone, as the locus of the stylistic battle between the formal and the informal. Instead, a landscape was the site of the interaction of people and place, and landscape architecture — exterior spatial design — the purposeful formation of that interaction.[1] By the time of the book's publication in 1950, Eckbo had secured a professional reputation of international scope. With a handful of colleagues, he had tested and pushed the limits of how landscape architecture was practiced and, perhaps more important, how it was conceived. By midcentury, landscape architecture could rightfully claim a modern, if not always a modernist, orientation.[2] Admittedly, this was almost five decades after modernism had transformed painting and sculpture, and three decades after its acceptance as a viable approach to architecture. The path had not been easy, and it had taken some unusual turns along the way. Garrett Eckbo's own path began in New York.

### Early Years

Eckbo was born in Cooperstown, New York, on 28 November 1910. His father possessed only limited business acumen and each of his proj-

Garrett Eckbo.
Los Angeles,
1959.
[*Julius Shulman*]

ects intended to advance the financial security of the family seemed to achieve just the opposite effect.[3] The result was a move west, first to Reno for his parents' divorce, and then to Alameda, California, with a new stepfather. Here the young Eckbo remained through his college years.

Growing up with "limited social opportunities," Eckbo says that he acquired both ambition and direction only after a half-year's stay in distant Norway with his paternal uncle, Eivind Eckbo, in 1929.[4] As he watched the economic and social success achieved through dedicated effort, Eckbo began to consider his options for the future, a future clouded shortly thereafter by the collapse of the international economy. He worked for two years as a bank messenger and at other jobs, attended Marin Junior College for a year, and entered the University of California in 1932. But what discipline should he study?

> So I went through the catalog and I found a subject, landscape design, I think it was called then, in the College of Agriculture. And I thought, well, I always used to like to play with plants in the garden, and my mother told me I was artistic, so maybe I should try this.[5]

When Garrett Eckbo entered the University of California, the landscape program was already four decades old. Frederick Law Olmsted had designed the original plan for the then College of California in 1865, when the nascent institution moved to Berkeley from Oakland to escape the corrupting influence of the city.[6] The College of Agriculture added a course in Landscape Gardening and Floriculture in 1913, with John W. Gregg as professor. Katherine Jones complemented Gregg's strengths and interests with an expertise in plant materials. The curriculum intended to provide "both theoretical and practical" instruction, leading toward professional competence. In manner, the program was neither innovative nor retrograde, neither blindly formal nor uncritically informal, educating its graduates at levels commensurate with the national standard. The collapse of the stock market in 1929 and the ensuing depression colored the role of the landscape architecture profession throughout the country, as estate design gave way to public parks, land reclamation, and water management.

More directly influential in the formation of Garrett Eckbo's thinking was H. Leland ("Punk") Vaughan, whose ideas about landscape architecture contrasted with those of the more senior members of the faculty. A fortuitous meeting with University of California alumnus Thomas Church at Ohio State, resulted in Vaughan's appointment to teach courses in construction, and implicitly, in design. Francis Violich, who graduated from Berkeley in 1934, wrote of Vaughan:

> *Vaughan (age 25) brought a younger generation's forward look-*
> *ing point of view that provided common ground with the stu-*
> *dents of those changing times. His broader European and East*
> *Coast experience, his understanding of land building relationship,*
> *his exposure to modern design ideas, all seemed to turn the*
> *department around.[7]*

Vaughan's presence thus stimulated in Berkeley students an open-minded vision that questioned the complacency of landscape practice in the Far West. He "emphasized economy and clear thinking in the design studio, not as a source of style but as examples of design reflecting time, place, and people."[8] The writings and work of Garrett Eckbo reflect many aspects of Vaughan's philosophy.

Thomas Church, who preceded Eckbo at Berkeley by about a decade, had seen in the Mediterranean countries a source of inspiration and pragmatic parallels to the California condition. Even before the turn of the century the myth of California's Spanish past had played an increasingly influential role in forming the state's architecture. Helen Hunt Jackson's *Ramona*, published in 1884, described the carefree outdoor life of Mexican-America, the vibrancy of the patio, and the fragrance of the night-blooming vines.[9] By the 1920s a Spanish Colonial Revival was well under way in California, given authority by a 1925 municipal ordinance in Santa Barbara that prescribed buildings in the central district to be designed in idioms recalling Andalusia and other Iberian locales.

In the hands of talented designers such as James Osborne Craig, Lutah Maria Riggs, and George Washington Smith, the Santa Barbara works turned out magnificently, using plays of solids and courtyards efficiently and to great effect.[10] While romantic shopping complexes such as Craig's 1923 El Paseo used meandering paths and architectural mood to evoke mythical memories of Spain, the city's and period's true monument was the Santa Barbara County Courthouse of 1928 by William Moser. In both instances, landscape elements strikingly complemented the architecture, with the red, magenta, or tawny hues of massive bougainvillea plantings staining the white brilliance of stuccoed walls.

Church's 1927 graduate thesis at Harvard was titled "A Study of Mediterranean Gardens and Their Adaptability to California Conditions," an announcement of Church's professional intentions after the requisite travel in Europe. Fortune brought Church and architect William Wurster together in the early 1930s, and together they developed buildings and landscape for the golf community of Pasatiempo near Santa Cruz. Despite his interest in the Mediterranean countryside, Church's work at Pasatiempo reflected the greatest respect for the native landscape, and his interventions with clipped plantings, lawns and beds, were quite restricted in both scale and exuberance.[11] Later in the decade, as his San Francisco practice began to flourish, Church's designs turned more elaborate, though still tending to rely on the established polite vocabulary of the Italian formal garden. Hedges and parterres of clipped boxwood, axial walkways, and nearly symmetrical dispositions paralleled the decorum of the architectural scheme. While the selection of native and subtropical plant species and a certain relaxed correctness characterized these garden designs, they were still heavily tinted by the manners of the Mediterranean past.

Eckbo recalls that although the University of California's landscape program tended toward a Beaux-Arts doctrine that applied formal ideas to institutional projects and informal ones to residential designs, Berkeley was just a bit too far from its continental sources to maintain true orthodox rigor.

> It was a practical, pragmatic philosophy. It was not as doctrinaire as I found later in the East. It was just oriented toward solving problems and preparing students to work in the world the way it was then. It was a limited world in terms of design sources or design inspiration and ideas, which came basically from the movement of the old Beaux-Arts system into the West, where because of the climatic changes and other kinds of local problems, it was forced to become more practical and to adapt.[12]

The power of the California landscape normally diminished the formality of any scheme, softening any overbearingly geometric planting arrangements with an acknowledgment of view and cognizance of sun and wind—a lesson that would never be neglected in Eckbo's designs.

Eckbo had little contact with contemporary currents in landscape design when he entered college, and no evidence suggests a greater awareness of them when he graduated. He took courses in drawing, plant materials, history and construction as well as studio, and emerged a skilled designer with festering ideas that extended beyond those of quotidian practice. With a wry, tongue-in-cheek title, Eckbo undermined the name of one assignment, if not the actual design [figure 1].[13] A gently undulating entrance road traversed the golf course, transformed into a formal approach to the parking court before the U-shaped country club. Each of the programmatic elements was addressed in a straightforward manner, but no big ideas transcended the assembly of parts.

Seen from today's perspective, a third-year student project, An Estate in the Manner of Louis XIV, might be taken as completely ironic — but it was executed in all seriousness [figure 2]. The design was carefully planned and resolved, and a building or colonnade actively terminated the three allées of the *trivium*. A court formed between them set off the main "château" in a manner reminiscent of the central zone of André le Nôtre's design for Vaux-le-Vicomte from the 1660s. "This was perhaps the best plan I did [as an undergraduate]…. I was very interested in history when I was at Berkeley, and I practically memorized the Italian gardens — it wasn't so easy to memorize the French."[14] The first impression of yet another reduced replica of Versailles dissipates with greater scrutiny. While the prevailing central organization, cross axial scheme, and diagonal allées of the *patte d'oie* hark back to the formal gardens of seventeenth-century France, Eckbo tweaked almost every element of the classical plan, as a mannerist, if not a modernist. Given the openness of the curriculum, the tenor of the American economy, his commissions executed within a year after graduation, and his subsequent social vision, this design remains a complete — and charming — anomaly.

A plan for a small garden for Edwin Snyder [figure 3] demonstrated that the recent graduate could operate competently in more than the classical mode, although the scheme possessed no truly distinctive elements.[15] In many respects the design reinvestigated ideas for

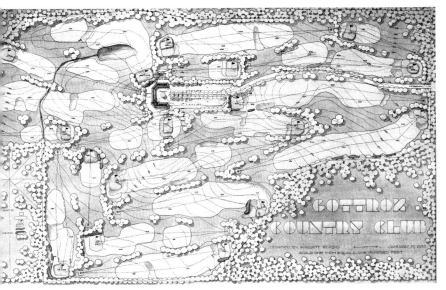

**1**

Gottrox Country Club,
Berkeley. Site plan.
Student project at the
University of California,
Berkeley, 1935.
Watercolor on paper.

[*Documents Collection*]

**2**

An Estate in the Manner of
Louis XIV. Aerial perspective.
Student project at the
University of California,
Berkeley, 1934.
Watercolor on paper.

[*Documents Collection*]

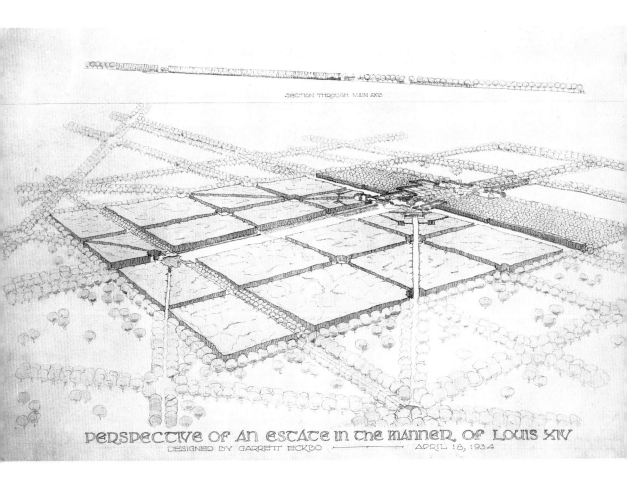

SECTION THROUGH MAIN AXIS

PERSPECTIVE OF AN ESTATE IN THE MANNER OF LOUIS XIV
DESIGNED BY GARRETT ECKBO ———————— APRIL 18, 1934

**3**
Snyder garden.
Rendered site plan.
Berkeley(?), 1935.
Pastel on diazo print.
[*Documents Collection*]

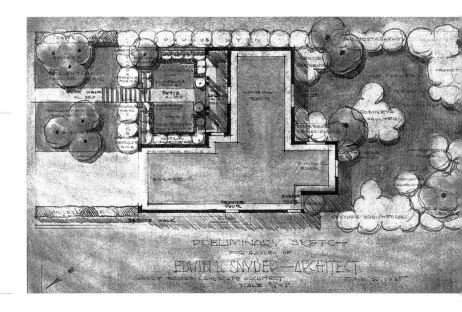

**4**
Esquisse for a Hillside
Garden. Site plan.
Student project at the
University of California,
Berkeley, 1933.
Ink on tracing paper.
[*Documents Collection*]

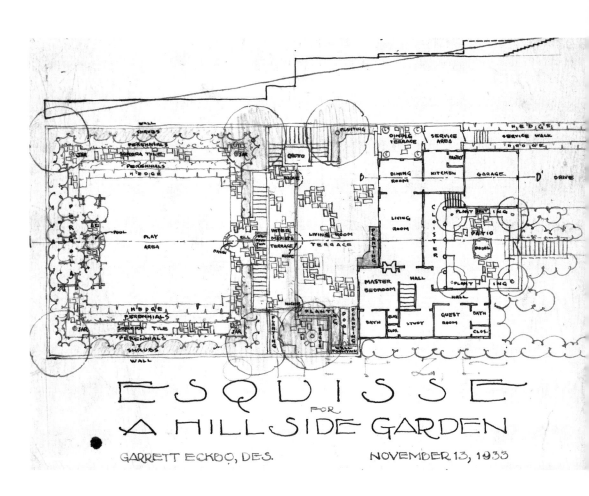

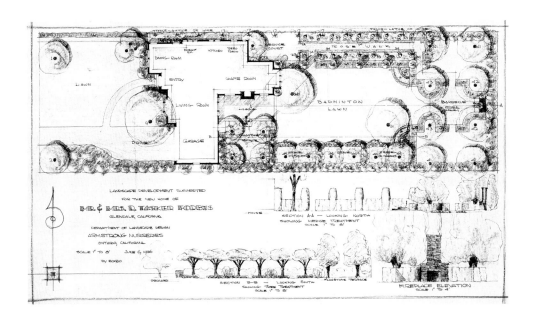

sequential zones characteristic of school projects such as the 1933 Esquisse for a Hillside Garden [figure 4], although its planting scheme was decidedly less rigid. A field of ground cover and two clumps of birches addressed the street, giving on to a rectangular enclosed patio that fronted the house's entry loggia. Masses of ceanothus and other shrubs disguised the borders of the lot to the rear and enveloped an exterior space that served as an extension of the living and dining rooms. Despite this early commission, the depression years were not a good time to enter private practice, and government work comprised almost all the available opportunities for landscape architects.[16] But John Gregg had helped arrange a job for Eckbo in Los Angeles and, a Bachelor of Science degree in hand, in summer 1935 the recent graduate headed south.

Los Angeles was hardly the sprawling, built-up, and smog-laden region it has come to be, and even today Eckbo retains only the fondest memories of his first years in the Southland paradise. He was employed by Armstrong Nurseries in Ontario to design gardens for its clients on sites ranging from the near-palatial to those of very modest dimensions. During his year working at the nursery, Eckbo designed about a hundred gardens, for which the average fee for

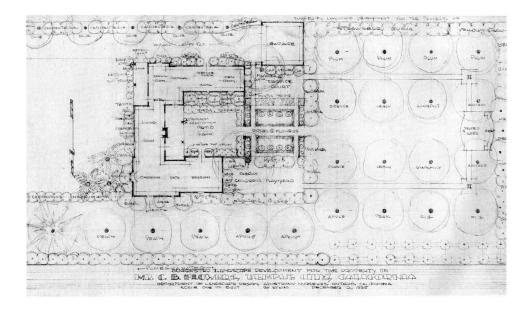

design was $10 — refunded with the client's first purchase of $25 worth of plants.[17] The drawings for many of these projects remain. As a group they suggest that the landscape architect had already begun to question the notion of styles applied indiscriminately to contemporary California. Set in these terms neither the formal axes of France and Italy, nor massed tree clumps of the English landscape garden, were appropriate to a dry suburban backyard. The schemes also illustrate that relaxed plantings and spaces were beginning to take hold in California, for example, in the work of H. L. and Adele Vaughan. While Eckbo claims that he "hadn't even heard the word modern in connection with landscape design" until he reached Harvard a year or so later, the Armstrong Nurseries designs clearly reflect a simplified organization and a softened formality that would become a strong part of modern landscape architecture.[18]

While we might kindly term these designs contemporary, in no way could they be termed modern. In many of them the flavor of the estate is brought down to the scale of the suburban house. A lawn politely announced the entrance, with shrubs defining the street edge, and trees such as sycamores dignifying the principal facade. The schemes also varied in their degree of formality, at times more rigor-

**6**
Flowers garden. Site plan. Temple City, 1935. Armstrong Nurseries. Pencil on tracing paper. [*Documents Collection*]

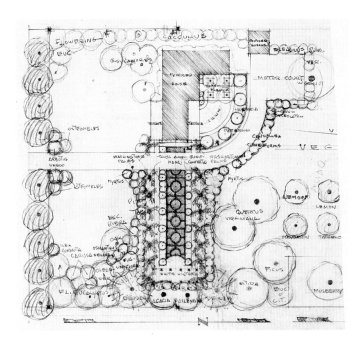

**7**
Garden design. Site plan.
Location unknown,
circa 1936.
Armstrong Nurseries.
Pencil on tracing paper.
[Documents Collection]

ously Moorish, at other times, more fuzzy [figure 5]. For larger sites, a motor court brought the car to the garage and visitors to the front door. Each of the outdoor work spaces — the drying yard and cutting garden, for example — were screened by shrubs, and defined exterior spaces to the south complemented the primary rooms of the house. The orchard, however minuscule, was a common element in many of these works. Although organized rigidly, these tended to be specimen orchards that might contain papaya, citrus, persimmon, orange, avocado, tangelo, and apple trees all in the same grid [figure 6]. Presumably the effect would be less ordered in the reality of maturing trees than in the simple uniform diameter circles shown on the plans, revealing certain contradictions within the design or naïveté on the part of the designer.

The overall planting, in fact, was varied and rich — one might say, overcomplicated and at times, even garish. The linear extension of the house in one unidentified garden design, for example, terminated in a pair of acacias, each flanked by a deodar cedar and announced by a splash of white wisteria — a curious combination of species, to say the least [figure 7]. In some instances the planting schemes ran riot, bringing to a single site lines of myrtle and ranges of eucalyptus.

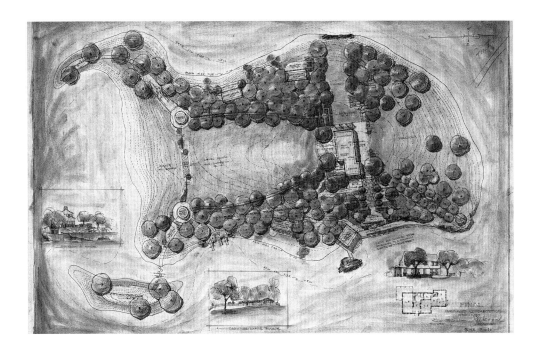

**8**
A Country Estate
on an Island.
Competition entry for
a Harvard University
scholarship, 1936.
Watercolor on paper.
[*Documents Collection*]

Whether this variety stemmed from the young Eckbo's desire to try out as many plants as he could, to see what the more benign (if necessarily irrigated) climate of southern California could uphold, or just reflected the fact that he was working for a nursery — which, after all was in the business of selling plants — we can only speculate.[19] But in his mature years Eckbo never matched in exuberance the planting schemes of his year at the Armstrong Nurseries. His later palette relied instead on an armature of greens enriched by varietals and well placed patches of color.

## Graduate Study

After less than a year of work, Eckbo could see that the horizons at the nursery were limited. The schemes were becoming "rote," and Eckbo was restless to expand his vision of landscape.[20] An opportunity for graduate study came his way by a scholarship competition sponsored by the Graduate School of Design at Harvard University. He entered the competition; he was successful. The winning design for a country estate on an island eschewed rigorous French or Italian formality, substituting instead a structured but less geometric development of the site [figure 8]. In the manner of Olmsted, or later

Fletcher Steele, the house was sited at the northern terminus of a broad lawn that linked the residence to the water. This greensward was leveled in the central area for "games" and gently bowed to exaggerate the sense of perspective from the shore up to the house. In the manner of the Italian Renaissance *bosco selvatico,* the wooded surroundings comforted a "casino" and outlook terrace; a more defined grassed swath opened eastward from the dining room, presumably for leisurely morning meals taken outdoors.

Eckbo acknowledges today that the design was "a fairly prosaic plan. There are probably twelve thousand gardens like this throughout the eastern part of the country. It has that kind of symmetrical informality that was begun at Mt. Vernon, which was the colonial period's contribution to ongoing design ideas."[21] But as a whole, the design was thoughtful and resolved. While the small sketches successfully illustrated the various architectural events on the island, neither the scheme nor its ink and watercolor rendering could match the brilliance of Eckbo's Beaux-Arts counterparts in France. But the entry was awarded first prize and secured for Eckbo a scholarship for further studies in landscape architecture. With his friend Francis Violich, Eckbo headed east, optimistic about the prospects of Ivy League education despite the lingering effects of the depression.

After a year at Harvard, and summer work in the Boston area, Eckbo traveled to New York to visit — and marry — Arline Williams [figure 9], the sister of his Berkeley classmate and future partner, Edward Williams.[22] During his first year of study, the graduate student found the curriculum superficially similar to that at Berkeley, and yet more rigidly entrenched. Henry Vincent Hubbard reigned as the theoretical head of the department, and the Beaux-Arts method formed the crux of his approach to design. The 1936 *Harvard University Register* defined landscape architecture as "primarily a fine art, which aims to create and preserve beauty in the efficient adaptation of land to human use."[23] Hubbard and Theodora Kimball's *Introduction to the Study of Landscape Design* codified this vision of landscape architecture and was regarded with near-reverence:

> *A work of art which has style may be esthetically organized in either of one of two fundamentally different ways. The artist may design his work to express his own ideas, to serve his own uses, to show his control over some of the materials and forces of*

**9**
Arline Williams.
Cambridge, Massachusetts,
1938.
[*Courtesy Arline Eckbo*]

*nature. Or on the other hand he may design his work to express*
*to the beholders the understanding which he has of some*
*modes of nature's organization, and the pleasure he finds in*
*them. In the first case, the esthetic success of the work will*
*require that the hand and the will of man be visible in it; in the*
*second case, the higher art would be that which so perfectly*
*interpreted nature's character that the work should seem to be*
*a wonderfully complete and intelligible expression of nature's*
*self.*[24]

As Eckbo remembers his Harvard education, its central issue was the
designer's visibility, usually expressed as the difference between the
informal and formal garden traditions. Most problems, he claims, were
stated in terms of that very broad dichotomy. And in his writings,
Eckbo hammered away at the false distinction between the formal
and informal modes while — ironically — dividing the world's garden
traditions into exactly those two categories. To him the particular
style in which a landscape was executed mattered less than the intention behind that vocabulary — which should not be a question of
style alone. In 1941, some three years after he received his master's
degree, he wrote:

*The formal garden forces architecture upon the landscape; the*
*informal garden forces the landscape upon architecture. Neither*
*does anything toward the basic problem of garden design: the*
*integration and harmonization of the structural geometry of man*
*with the biological growth and freedom of nature. This can't be*
*done by holding them apart and calling one formal and the*
*other informal. The fundamental fallacy seems to be that a*
*choice between the two extremes is necessary. The argument*
*has been to take either biology or geometry; why not biology*
*plus geometry?*[25]

Eckbo's telling of the story was based on a useful form of simplifi-
cation. In fact, as Reuben Rainey demonstrates, the Beaux-Arts
approach was more subtle than the modernists made it. Rarely was
any project entirely formal or entirely informal; almost always the
rigidity of any scheme would need be softened by the particularities
of the site and program.[26] While perhaps propelled to a greater
degree by a geometric structure, the formality of the garden scheme
was tempered and enriched by climate, plant materials, and the client.

Like any theoretical stance, this method was never as fixed as its opponents believed it to be; the presentation of the Beaux-Arts beliefs by Hubbard and Kimball was intelligent, comprehensive, and accepting of infinite manipulation and variation. To the graduate student, it didn't seem that way at the time. Eckbo's own copy of Hubbard and Kimball is filled with argumentative marginal notes that spoke back to the authority represented by the text.[27] While transparently the churlish cartooning of a prior era by the hand of its successor, these jottings reveal just how seriously Eckbo took his education, and how seriously he set the course for a modern landscape architecture.

However one may qualify Eckbo's caricatured retelling of his days at Harvard, there is no question that landscape pedagogy lagged well behind that of the architecture program. Joseph Hudnut had become the dean of the newly formed Graduate School of Design in 1935, bringing with him ideas about modernism and a renovated curriculum. "Our exigent problem is that of our place in the world," Hudnut wrote. "If indeed architecture can exist amidst airplanes, dynamos and motion pictures, it must seek a reconciliation with them, discovering a new grace and order in the very heart of contemporary technical processes."[28] Under Hudnut's invitation, the former Bauhaus director Walter Gropius came to Harvard in 1937 and, with Marcel Breuer, injected forefront European ideas about architecture and its social role into an American context. This connection, more than any issue of style, is what Eckbo would carry away from his courses in the architecture department: the link between society and what he would later term "spatial design." While landscape design embraces "surfacing, enclosure, enrichment," a designer strives to "give the richest, most plastic and satisfying form to the space which is being organized; the other is to concentrate always on that space as an arena, volume background, and shelter for human life and activity."[29]

For Gropius, "the term 'design' broadly embraces the whole orbit of man-made, visible surroundings, from simple everyday goods to the complex pattern of the whole town." Critics had questioned, with good reason, the Modernist project's efficacy in designing cities. Tellingly, there was no instruction in landscape architecture at the

Bauhaus. Eckbo's concern for art and science paralleled those advanced by Gropius and other architects who saw the need for creatively addressing new materials, standardization, and rationalized fabrication. "Good planning," wrote Gropius, "I conceive to be both a science and an art. As a science, it analyzes human relationships; as an art, it co-ordinates human activities into a cultural thesis."[30] This last sentence alone could have served as the basis for Eckbo's forthcoming master's thesis project.

In addition to the other European émigrés, Hudnut also invited the Canadian-English landscape architect Christopher Tunnard to teach at the Graduate School of Design. In 1934, recently graduated from the Royal Horticultural Society school at Wisley and the Westminster Technical Institute, he began to publish a series of articles in the journal of the Landscape Institute, and later the *Architectural Review*. Tunnard sought not only a modern manner for landscape design, but more profoundly, an approach that would avoid questions of style altogether. He, too, acknowledged that landscape history had fallen into considerations of formal and informal, but he found in Japan the "empathetic" manner by which a concern for the social and ecological landscape could transcend the very question of style: "This conception of Nature and natural forms finds one of its expressions in Japan (and it is beginning to in Europe) in the unity of the habitation with its environment."[31] Tunnard's essays ranged in subject matter from investigations into British landscape history to the use of sculpture in gardens, and were collected and published in 1938 as *Gardens in the Modern Landscape*. The tract would remain the sole English-language polemic for landscape modernism until the publication of Eckbo's own (and more comprehensive) *Landscape for Living* in 1950.

That Tunnard sought to draw landscape design into tandem with architecture and other modern arts underscored his belief that landscape architecture must be a social art as well as a social science. While the implicit argument for an expression in accord with the times is buried in the text, he rooted his argument in reason, history, and problem solving. Indeed, in an article published during the war years, Tunnard proposed that "the right style for the twentieth century is no style at all, but a new conception of planning the human environment." As James Rose had suggested several years before, Tunnard proposed modern architecture as the role model for a contemporary approach to landscape design: "Modern landscape design is inseparable from the spirit, technique, and development of modern architecture."[32] Clearly, the emerging generation saw its future in parallel with architecture rather than with the more specific investigations of painting and sculpture. While the latter almost always stood far in advance of the "social arts" — and avant-garde — in most instances they lacked a client, a program, and space — all requisites of landscape design.

Although locked into a more ossified theoretical stance than its architecture counterpart, the landscape program at the Graduate School of Design allowed its students the latitude to take courses in other subject areas and strike out on their own in both formulating and designing landscapes of their choosing — or at least subvert their studio assignments. Certain of Eckbo's projects were controlled by a formality not totally foreign to the work he had produced at Berkeley or during his year at the Armstrong Nurseries. By this time, however, narrow columns of explanatory text began to accompany each assignment, as a sort of sermon on landscape theory. For one project for a country estate, the notes read:

> A country estate: a place where people live in the country; in intimate and sympathetic relation with the landscape; areas used by man, formed by man in an intelligent and unashamed manner. Areas unused by man left natural. Developed and undeveloped areas concentrated so as to achieve maximum effect from each, and contrast of two together. A forecourt is a reception room for automobiles, let it be an extension of the house, not an approach to it. People like to dine out of doors, swim and play tennis in gay surroundings, sit and walk in the shade, and look out on a pleasant, spacious view.[33]

**10**
Freeform Park,
Washington, D.C.
Partial site/planting plan.
Student project at Harvard
University, 1937.
Pencil on tracing paper.
[Documents Collection]

The estate's design continued the long tradition of more formally planned areas — forecourts, terraces, and orchards — set against the naturalistic order of the woods, in essence, continuing the play between geometrically and informally planned zones.

If these early assignments suggested a wavering between what he had learned at Berkeley and what he was acquiring through his

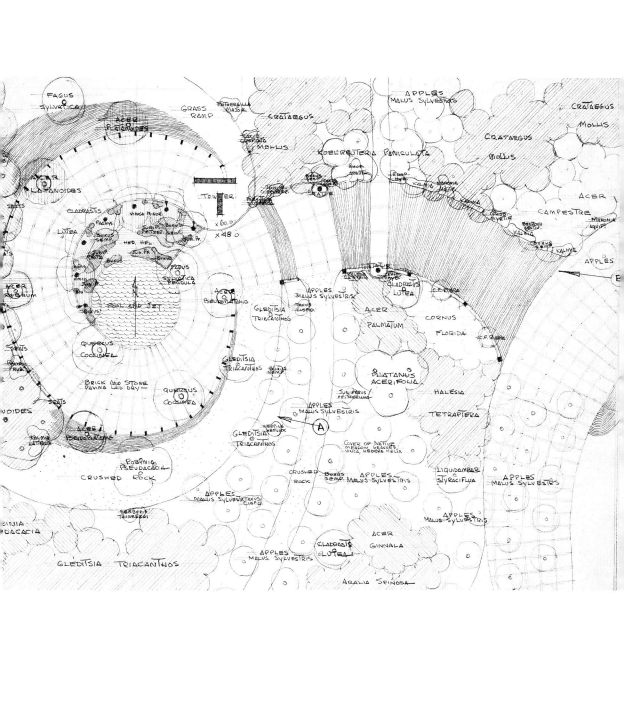

architectural forays at Harvard, the design for a Freeform Park in Washington, D.C., left no question about his future direction.[34] The overall planning of the island site in the Potomac was asymmetrically developed, heavily weighted toward its western tip [see plate I]. The approach road cut northward across the island before veering west toward the park's central space. Here, tree plantings spiraled toward a round pool at the plaza's center flanked by a tower made of two concrete slabs (architecture student friends helped Eckbo on the design) [figures 10, 11]. London plane trees prevailed, lining the edge of the road and enclosing the plaza. A grid of ornamental apple trees (*Malus sylvestris*) was planted as a foil for the roads and for clumps of locusts and maples.

The note accompanying the rendered site plan dispelled any doubt about the author's patriotic and artistic intentions behind the design:

> *A memorial to the fathers of our country in which the informal becomes modern, modern goes informal, but a tree remains a tree. The topographical spirit of the island is preserved insofar as possible: a low ridge, from which one looks out and down. The bell tower is a structure of reinforced concrete, steel, and glass, which substitutes lightness, grace, and openness for the monumental tombstone effect. Tree masses used to relate tower to the island and define movement of circulation.*[35]

Even at this early date, we see Eckbo bristling against the simple bifurcation of approaches to landscape into the informal and the formal, and to the application — however updated — of received ideas. Instead, he was searching for a new vocabulary, a vocabulary like the International style in architecture, to announce the arrival of modernity. More important, this idiom would signal a new regard for landscape architecture *in* society. His search sought sources in architecture, painting, and sculpture.

## The New Space of the Garden

Modern architecture suggested that space was the most important aspect of landscape or architectural design. As Eckbo later wrote in *Landscape for Living*, when we purchase a lot, we are actually buying a block of space — why be concerned with only the design of its surface [figure 12]? Spatial design is achieved through both inert and

11
Freeform Park, Washington, D.C. Sketch of the tower. Student project at Harvard University, 1937.
Pencil on tracing paper.
[*Documents Collection*]

vegetal materials, and seen in this light, the quests of architecture and landscape are actually congruent. That one discipline produced roofed space and the other spaces open to the sky, to Eckbo was no viable reason for this artificial division. In truth, both professions shared a common goal: a landscape for living, if landscape be taken in much broader terms to include people and their relationship to the land.[36]

Eckbo shared this interest in space with the architects of his generation and with his landscape classmates as well. James Rose would become one of modern landscape architecture's most polemical writers during the 1940s, beginning to publish almost as soon as he left school. In the 1938 article "Freedom in the Garden," for example, Rose, like Eckbo, noted the affinity between landscape design and sculpture. What distinguished the two, however, was the focus on space: "In reality, [landscape design] is outdoor sculpture, not to be looked at as an object, but designed to surround us in a pleasant sense of space relations."[37] Using illustrations of drawings by Picasso, houses by Mies van der Rohe, and sculpture by Naum Gabo — paired with images of his own projects — Rose sought parallels in the arts to propel developments in landscape architecture.

In *The International Style*, Henry-Russell Hitchcock and Philip Johnson advanced a concern for space over mass as a defining characteristic of modern architecture. Like Frank Lloyd Wright's citing of Taoism and in particular Lao Tzu in "the reality of the vessel is the space within," the formation of space and the use of space by human beings became central issues in Eckbo's work.[38] His appreciation of Ludwig Mies van der Rohe's 1929 German Pavilion in Barcelona was obvious in his writings and in his designs, in particular the use of the overlapping rather than intersecting corner. And in projects ranging from suburban backyards to expansive housing estates, plant materials and constructed planes were first and foremost addressed to defining space. The forms by which space was delimited followed closely thereafter.

But what of the particular vocabulary that would form the modern landscape? To appear contemporary one might investigate the most free of aesthetic investigations: painting and sculpture. In an early article, "Sculpture & Landscape Design," published just as he was com-

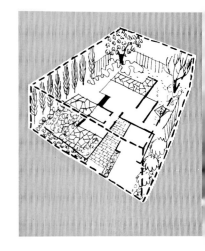

12
"Your Block of Air."
Carlos Diniz, delineator.
[*from Garrett Eckbo*, The Art of Home Landscaping]

pleting graduate studies, Eckbo stressed the intrinsic connection between architecture, landscape, and the plastic arts. Although emphasizing the essential unity of the arts, he cautioned that "landscape design concerns itself with provision for the outdoors activities of man."

> Architecture [like sculpture]… works with three-dimensional volumes, but their arrangement is governed by human activities which they must shelter.… Yet sculpture is also analogous to landscape design, for the handling of ground masses can be carried out with a truly sculptural sense of forms in relation. In fact, landscape design may be considered more analogous to sculpture, since its forms are moulded and carved and grouped, whereas those in architecture are constructed.[39]

Alfred Barr, founding director of the Museum of Modern Art, had analyzed the development of abstraction in painting and sculpture and distinguished between "pure-abstraction" and "near-abstraction": "Pure-abstractions are those in which the artist makes a composition of abstract elements such as geometrical or amorphous shapes. Near-abstractions are compositions in which the artist, starting with natural forms, transforms them into abstract or nearly abstract forms."[40] This dichotomy opened a conceptual application of the contemporary plastic arts to landscape design, suggesting to designers their role as the designers of habitable near-abstractions.

Barr included architecture, film, furniture, graphic, and theater design in his exhibition "Cubism and Abstract Art," but landscape architecture was notably absent, as it had been from the Bauhaus.[41] Yet even in this century, garden designers — often architects or interior designers rather than landscape architects — had explored the links between the aesthetic zeitgeist and outdoor space. Most obvious was the "cubistic" idiom of Gabriel Guevrekian's Garden of Water and Light at the 1925 Exposition Internationale des Arts Décoratifs et Industriels Modernes in Paris, and his walled garden for the Villa Noailles in Hyères executed three years later. The landscape profession was introduced to the French work through publications — all in French and virtually linguistically inaccessible to the young Americans, with the notable exception of Fletcher Steele's 1930 "New Pioneering in Garden Design." Eckbo was so impressed with a view of Pierre-Émile

13
Pierre-Émile Legrain.
Tachard garden.
La Celle-Saint-Cloud,
France, circa 1924.
Sketch by Garrett Eckbo
from a photo.
[Courtesy Garrett Eckbo]

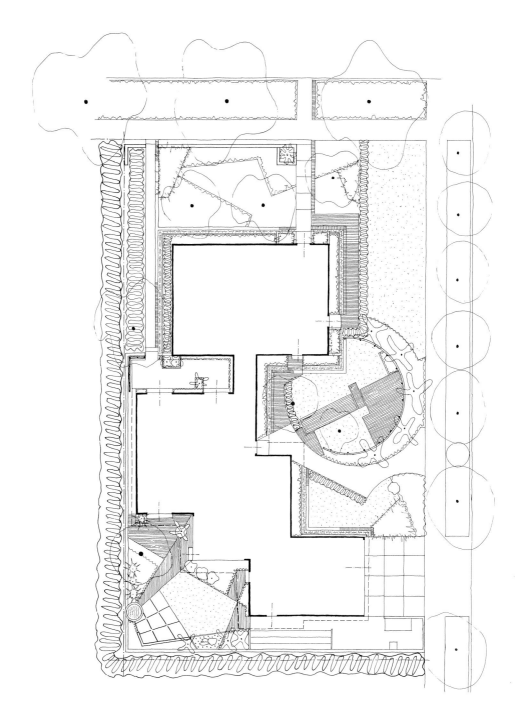

**14**
Jones garden. Site plan.
Ontario, late 1940s(?).
Ink on tracing paper.

[*Documents Collection*]

Legrain's Tachard garden in La Celle-Saint-Cloud, he overlaid the
photo to produce his own sketch for further study [figure 13].

> It blew my mind because of that little sawtooth edge, which you
> probably think is kind of silly, but it made me think about what a
> path is for. A straight path with straight sides is a linear move-
> ment through space, designed to get you from here to there as
> quickly as possible. It's like a street or highway. But if you break
> the edge like that, you say that there's something along the side
> that maybe you should stay and look at. It was a form that
> came out of modern art.[42]

While the zigzag path rarely maximized its effect on movement in the
Eckbo garden, it became one of the landscape architect's favored
design motifs. And the influence of the banked earthen planes — in
pattern, if not actual form — of Guevrekian's Garden of Water and
Light and Legrain's Tachard garden are most obvious in Eckbo's
studies for the segmented patterning of the Jones garden (Ontario,
undated, probably late 1940s) [figure 14; see plate IV].

As a graduate student, Eckbo was well aware of developments in the
arts, and the bibliographies of his articles and books balance read-
ings in the arts with sociology, soil conservation, and planning. In
"Sculpture & Garden Design," which appeared in the Magazine of Art
in 1938, his setting for a modern sculpture reworked the spiral row
of trees that enclosed the plaza of his Freeform Park project. But
here the motif had been adapted for purely aesthetic ends. Intended
to terminate the allée of a large garden, the design's "ramped earth

planes meet at a low mound, from which rises a piece of modern
sculpture whose smooth forms blend readily with the earth forms."
Archipenko's *Hero* became the central feature of the design, an image
appropriated from Alfred H. Barr's *Cubism and Abstract Art* first published in 1936.[43] This borrowing was no doubt intended to add a
gloss of modernity to the design's vegetal elements. In any event, the
article's publication offered Eckbo a national arena in which to broad-
cast his views — certainly among the earliest exposures of modern
landscape to the American public.

Eckbo was not alone in his quest for a modern landscape architecture. His Harvard classmates included James Rose and Dan Kiley, and
the trio would come to play a pivotal role in twentieth-century
American landscape architecture [figures 15, 16].[44] Given their callow
youth and radical ideas, it is startling that the band found a forum for
their writings so early on, and that they chose to attack global problems and theories rather than small-scale garden design issues alone.
In 1939–40, they jointly published a series of articles that laid out an
approach to design based on a three-part division of the earth into
primeval (i.e., wilderness), rural, and urban landscapes. Citing Lewis
Mumford in the essay on design in the primeval landscape, they
asserted that it is impossible to design responsibly in any of the three
arenas without considering — and affecting — the remaining two. In
closing, they stressed that "the design principles underlying the planning of the urban, rural and primeval environments are identical: use
of the best available means to provide for specific needs of the specific inhabitants; this results in specific forms."[45]

**17**

James C. Rose, Bibby estate. Kingston, New York. Student project at Harvard University, 1938.

*[from James C. Rose, "New Freedom in Garden Design"]*

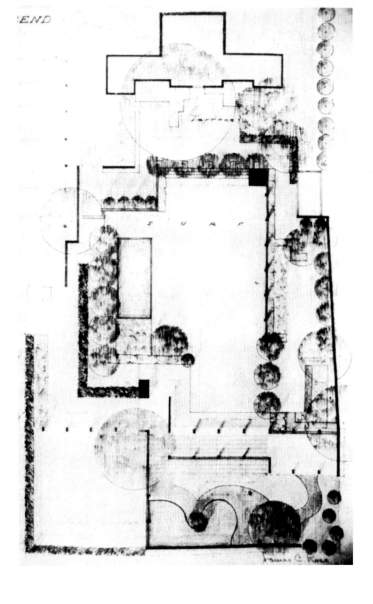

**18**

Pablo Picasso. *Figure*, 1910.

*[from James C. Rose, "New Freedom in Garden Design"]*

Perhaps not surprisingly, it was the architecture journals that gave space to Rose and Eckbo for their writings. In "Freedom in the Garden" Rose argued for a landscape design that was spatially based, which he illustrated with modern architecture, painting, and sculpture as well as his own projects. The images were used rhetorically. A plan of his 1938 Harvard school project for the Bibby estate in Kingston, New York, was paired with *Figure*, a drawing by Pablo Picasso [figures 17, 18]. Other examples were drawn from the work of Theo van Doesburg, Mies van der Rohe, and Naum Gabo. In projects undertaken as a graduate student, Rose clearly demonstrated his comprehension of modernist architecture, as he applied its notions of spatial fluidity to the garden. In 1940 he wrote that "we are already accustomed to a freer type of space organization — living/dining rooms with groups arranged for conversation, study, and play....We have yet to develop the house and landscape unit on the same basis rather than just the house with the garden attached."[46]

Although a socially reinvigorated landscape architecture adapted its aesthetic vocabulary from contemporary plastic arts, underlying both was the spirit of the times — and a belief in progress and most of all the positive rational power of science. Science and the promise of technology in realizing the democratic ideal were frequent themes in both Rose's and Eckbo's writings. Gropius had written that the new architecture derived not from the personal aesthetic tics of a handful of designers but "simply the inevitable logical product of the intellectual, social and technical conditions of our age."[47]

Vaguely defined and open to a variety of interpretations, the positive impact of technology ran as a common thread in publications by various authors on landscape design. Tunnard wrote about science in 1938, restricting his purview to the development of hybrid species and the improvement of the soil:

> Just as the design of the locomotive, the aeroplane, and, for that matter, the modern house, is being changed by scientific invention, in a similar way, science will transform the garden of the future. The latter must necessarily be influenced by new materials and their methods of application — for example, by plant importation and hybridization, and the amelioration of soil and weather conditions.[48]

Rose pushed the matter further but diverted the topic of discussion in his 1939 article "Why Not Try Science?" He bemoaned the fact that landscape thinking lagged so far behind developments in architecture, hampered by the employ of traditional building materials and plant varieties. Science was not an abstract idea, he claimed, but instead directed the landscape architect's working method. More specifically — and surprisingly — a scientific use of plants meant avoiding plants used in masses: "It is only by the isolation of specimens that plants can be controlled scientifically, developed to the ultimate of their potential characteristics, and used with elastic tensility. It is the method employed in all scientific investigation in horticulture — and in the study of building materials." In fact, if science has anything to demonstrate, wrote Rose, "it has proved that so-called 'natural' conditions are not necessarily the best conditions for development." Having dismissed the emulation of nature as impossible, Rose made absolutely no apologies for his view:

> It is perfectly possible to use plants with the same knowledge and efficiency with which we use lumber, brick, steel, or concrete in building. And when we apply the science of growth to our landscape design standards, so that we can determine accurately the form characteristics and definitely establish the growth rates for individual plants under given conditions, we will be able to use plants with the same expediency as the factory-made, modular unit in building.[49]

The influence of modern architecture on Rose's thinking appears to have been decisive, no doubt inculcated by his training under Gropius. Curiously, Rose offered no more than broad notions of landscapes appropriate to contemporary living; he rarely spoke of the specific use or user group for these landscapes. His concern fell almost completely on spatial and formal ideas, with few specific notions of people, modern thinking — or science.

## Science

By the time *Landscape for Living* was published, Eckbo's view of science had been greatly modified. In the immediate postwar era, with the world again free for democracy, almost everything seemed possible. Technology reappeared as a fully positive force and, with it, the optimism witnessed at the 1939 World's Fair in New York. In the introduction to *Landscape for Living*, "Why Now," Eckbo announced his desire for "a serious analysis, in terms of theory and practice, of landscape development in our culture." The advance of the scientific method in all fields of inquiry, including less "exact" fields "such as esthetics and sociology" occasioned this study: "The scientific method is one which takes nothing for granted, accepts no precedents without examination, and recognizes a dynamic world in which nothing is permanent but change itself." Thus, to Eckbo, science was less a force or a body of knowledge than a stance by which to re-examine his discipline, landscape architecture. He quoted Christopher Cauldwell: "Art is the science of feeling, science the art of knowing. We must know to be able to do, but we must feel to know what to do." Put into Eckbo's own terms, this is the difference between "know-how" and "know-why:" "Theory is the why of doing things, practice is the how. If practice is know-how, theory is know-why. Theory must serve practice; must answer the questions raised by practice; and must be tested by the data of practice."[50] Seen in these terms, theory and practice are complementary, helping landscape architecture — which becomes a humanistic science — create appropriate outdoor settings for human existence. This theme recurs through almost all of Eckbo's writings, reflecting — if not as forcefully — the conviction with which he advanced it in *Landscape for Living*.

The call for a scientific method for landscape architecture raised questions as to its manifestation as garden form and space. On the one hand, designers hold *conceptual* interests that address broader, almost intangible, issues such as "contemporary living," "technology," and "science." These rarely find a direct, perceivable expression in any landscape design and serve primarily to propel the designer in his or her work. Thus, these factors tend to color the values behind the design but lack a direct expression within it. On the other hand, the *perceptual* concerns demand an expression appropriate to the designer's values and aesthetic sensibility. It was at this level that investigations in the other arts were so important for the development of the modern garden in California. Shapes, forms, and spaces drawn from the work of Pablo Picasso, Georges Braque, Wassily Kandinsky [figure 19], Mies van der Rohe, László Moholy-Nagy [figure 20], Naum Gabo, El Lizzitsky, Joan Miró, Jean Arp, and Isamu Noguchi

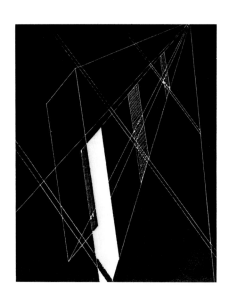

were as important for what they were not as for what they were: they were neither the informal nor the formal tradition. Instead their idiom spoke of today, of design in space.[51]

## Painting, Sculpture, and Landscape Design

More significantly perhaps, modern painting signaled the arrival of non-perspectival space, an idea with which landscape designers could counter the thrust of the formal axis or the informal clump. Joan Miró spoke of the "motionless movement" he sought in painting, another idea with possible application to the new garden: "As there is no horizon line nor indication of depth, [the forms] are displaced in depth. They are also displaced in plane, because a colour or a line leads fatally to a displacement of the angle of vision. Inside the large forms, small forms move. And, when you look at the whole picture, the large forms become mobile in turn."[52]

Denied the picture plane, painting could become a space without areal boundaries and possessing infinite depth, undermining the reading of the painting as a representation with ties to the objective world. The space and movement of a landscape employing the elements of nonobjective painting — here turned into "nonobjective spaces" — could better accommodate contemporary living outdoors. The years at Harvard constituted a pivotal stage in Eckbo's formation; and academic study gave him a laboratory for pure research and its applied development. Several design studies investigated the linkage of modern art with Eckbo's more socially rooted ideas.

The 1937 project for, and subsequent publication of, "Small Gardens in the City" functioned as an advanced manifesto for the urban landscape [figure 21]. The undertaking was entirely self-motivated, intended to serve as a near-culmination to his graduate study — a thesis would follow — and a testing of ideas concerning the elements of a modern urban landscape.[53] Eckbo developed the design of eighteen gardens on a single city block, patterned in dimension on the urban units of San Francisco with which he was so familiar: "This was a study of design possibilities — a study of physical form, based on the idea that the content would develop over time."[54] The architecture of the houses to complement the gardens was more or less assumed and in the end mattered little in terms of the site design — other than the functional connection between indoor and outdoor spaces.

**19**
Wassily Kandinsky.
*Composition I,* 1921.
[*Yale University Art Gallery*]

**20**
László Moholy-Nagy.
*Composition no. 4,* 1923–24.
[*Katherine S. Dreier Bequest, ©1996 Museum of Modern Art, New York*]

The site sloped slightly, affording minimal opportunities to sculpt the terrain. The gardens—presented in model form as an entirety and individually as axonometric ink drawings—developed variations on particular themes [figure 22a-d]. Some designs seem to have begun with the limits of the site and worked inward; others expanded outward from the living spaces of the house. The thrust of the designs varied from those aligned with the shape of the lot, to those turned obliquely to the walls, to those using a less geometric idiom as a means to distance the garden from the rectangular bonds of the lot. In one garden, arc segments descended the slope in overlapping terraces; another employed a geometry rotated 45 degrees to the edges of the site. The modeled ground plane acquired a third dimension, and considerable tracts of paving complemented areas of low vegetation and ground covers. Tree plantings were arranged more freely, in places appearing more as sculptural elements than as providers of shade and mass. Pergolas and other light structures completed the designer's palette.

With all their innovation and individual formal brilliance, the eighteen gardens created little sense of a continuous landscape; they remained discretely conceived and bounded. Only in certain minor gestures— like the zigzag fence that traversed the property limits—did Eckbo challenge the tyranny of the lot line.[55] The street side of each house was left untouched. Like a botanical garden, with each plot assigned to a different plant family, each unit tested a varied formal vocabulary but left the greater question of the urban landscape conglomerate unquestioned. Eckbo would address this issue in his thesis, Contempoville, completed the following year.

Conceived as an independent school project, "Small Gardens in the City" was published within six months of its completion in *Pencil Points*, one of the United States' leading architectural journals. Taking stock of his audience, Eckbo wrote an explanatory text, laying the ground rules for the small bounded site and elucidating the assumptions behind his investigations. He cited his original thoughts and added an updated commentary in a 1993 memoir:

> "Gardens are places in which people live out of doors."

> "Gardens must be the homes of delight, of gaiety, of fantasy, of illusion, of imagination, of adventure." These

**21**
Small Gardens in the City.
Model.
Student project at Harvard University, 1937.
[*Documents Collection*]

**22a–d**
Small Gardens in the City.
Axonometric studies.
Student project at Harvard
University, 1937.
Ink on tracing paper.
[*Documents Collection*]

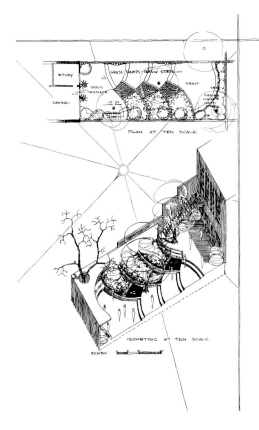

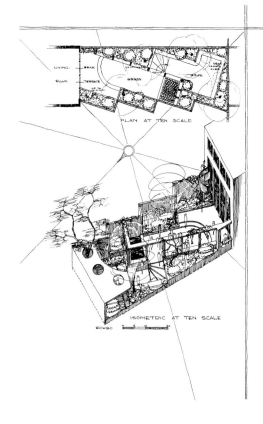

**a**

*Abstraction of natural con-
tours, curved terraces follow
nature slope. Curves need be
neither "naturalistic" nor "formal." Any garden made by
man is formed, therefore formal. Outside connection of
garden with second-story living room is very important
to unity of house and garden
and circulation.*

**b**

*Spatial design. Shape of an
area warped to break up
feeling of hard enclosure.
Colonnade gives distance by
partial concealment and
enframement of lower end
of garden. Ample planting
space. Change in property
line by agreement between
two owners.*

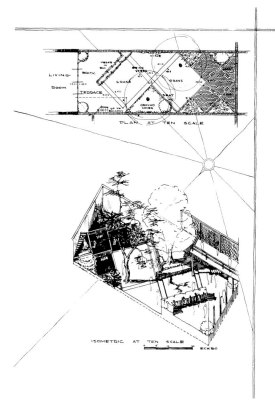

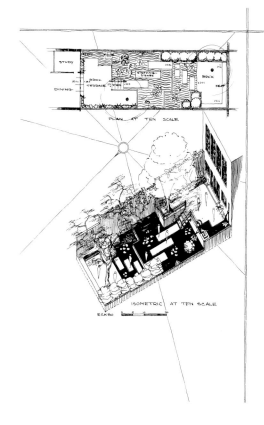

**c**

Repetition of a simple
square turned at a 45-
degree angle. Line of descent
follows natural slope. Plants
as specimens. Water either
moving or still. Abstraction of
natural forms; the spirit, not
the semblance.

**d**

Water garden. Population of
aquatics, fish, frogs, and tur-
tles. Thrill of crossing by stepping stones to lower sitting
area. Pattern from second-
story living room.

*are not physical qualities. The assumption was that bold and free arrangements of space and material would generate such feelings and responses.*

*"Designs shall be three-dimensional. People live in volumes, not planes."*

*"Designs shall be areal, not axial."… Spatial experience is more than a line.*

*"Design shall be dynamic, not static."… Axial design tends to be static, its obvious purpose being to express and freeze the status quo. We do not want to live in a static world.[56]*

With his graduate studies still uncompleted, Eckbo had already received validation through publications in leading art and design journals.

### Collective Landscapes

During his time at Harvard, Eckbo collaborated with architects and planners, sowing the seeds for his continuing interest in the greater sphere beyond the limits of the individual lot and garden. A project for a recreation center in South Boston, designed with architecture students Saunders, Robinson, Currie, and Crain, suggested the superstructure for public space assigned to varied use.[57] This expanded scope of inquiry was further developed in his thesis study Contempoville, which portrayed Eckbo's vision for the ideal American suburb: a subdivision linked to an imagined 1945 world's fair in Los Angeles. Troubled by the valuing of individual expression over community good, Eckbo proposed a total landscape linked by pervasive rows of hedges reinforced by tall trees [figure 23]. Each family received its own domestic compound, each its privacy ensured by untrimmed hedges. Each site acknowledged its boundaries and yet appeared to develop centrifugally from the interior of the house. The planning idea held consistently throughout, yet Eckbo again used a remarkable variety of formal vocabularies for the designs of the gardens. Oval beds; skewed plantings of hedges; networks of interlocking paths — all these ground patterns were complemented by the higher masses and canopies of trees, composing the domestic space outdoors in three spatial levels. Eckbo's explanatory text read:

**23**
Contempoville.
Study for the overall
site plan.
Student project at Harvard
University, 1938.
Ink on tracing paper.
[*Documents Collection*]

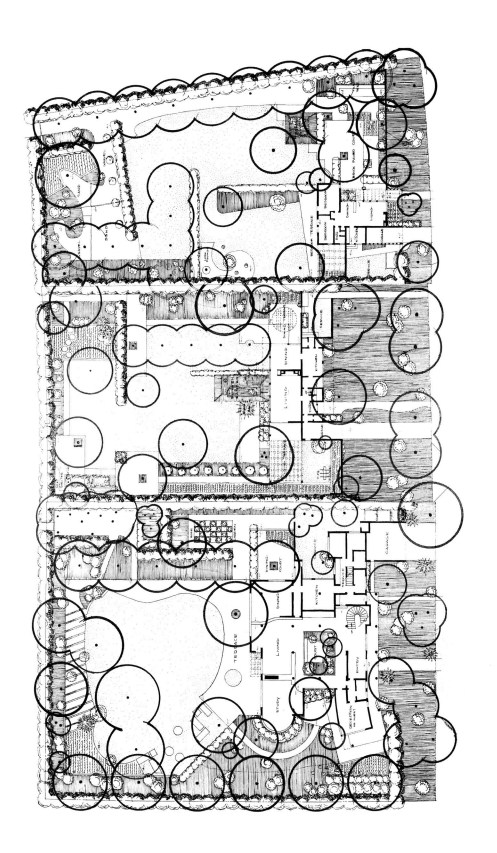

*House and garden developed as an organic unit which will present a compelling setting for the "more abundant life." The garden flows into the house; the house reaches out into the garden.... Nature will dominate these gardens because the plant material is so placed that it can continue its growth with a minimum of interference by the hand of man.*[58]

This statement is remarkably prescient in summarizing Eckbo's regard for the single-family site and its relation to the community, and the relation of planned nature to its maintenance and growth.

Contempoville's layout employed the winding roads common to the American suburb, with a central park area that could be traced back to the common of colonial times. The suburb's subdivision and design, however, clearly reflected more advanced planning ideas, such as those of Clarence Wright and Henry Stein. Each of the house plans were designed by "real architects" and taken from professional publications;[59] the Barcelona Pavilion made a cameo appearance as the social center of the plan, its reflecting pool adapted for the more mundane function of swimming. The structure's flowing spaces were joined to an amphitheater on one side by sinuous plantings of hedges; a tennis court abutted the buildings' eastern walls. Given the age of its designer, and the scope of his landscape designs executed until this time, the project evinced an astonishing cohesion from site plan to detailed garden plans. The specific vocabulary employed at Contempoville would be loosened in the succeeding decades. But in many respects — foremost among them the ideas of linkage, the group, and the individual home — would stay as constant foundations for almost all of Eckbo's community plans.

Although Contempoville was a more comprehensive and ultimately more significant exercise, it was the Small Gardens in the City project that announced to the architectural readership Eckbo's arrival as a professional with advanced ideas about modern landscape design. Its republication in France, and its inclusion in Margaret Olthof Goldsmith's 1941 *Designs for Outdoor Living*, reiterated the power of the ideas and the hunger for a new view of landscape architecture.[60] In some ways, Eckbo seems to have already cut his connections with landscape architecture as it had been conceived and as it was prac-

**24**
Garrett Eckbo
in cap and gown.
Harvard University
Commencement, 1938.
[*Documents Collection*]

ticed. Here was a vision more compressed and fitted to contemporary conditions and aesthetic developments, aimed at the city more
than the estate of the wealthy client. Eckbo's use of publications
reveals an incredible drive for soap-boxing, self-promotion, and astute
utilization of the print medium. Indeed, he would become a prolific
writer, with six books and countless articles published over half a century.

## A Graduate Again

Through Frederick Gutheim, whom Eckbo met at Harvard, Mr. Eckbo
went to Washington [figure 24]. His courtyard plans for the United
States Housing Authority were less specific solutions to specific problems than studies that tested the range of possibilities for developing
exterior recreational space [see figure 86]. We see here the further-
ing of the Contempoville and Small Gardens ideas, or the selective
adoption of elements first proposed there to define spaces for sitting,
conversation, light work, and play (on the drawings termed "pre-
school: active; adult: passive"). By applying the spatial ideas of buildings
such as the Barcelona Pavilion [figure 25] — in which walls slide past
one another, Eckbo created fluid spaces assigned to specific purposes, without sacrificing a sense of the whole. Vegetation was restricted,
its use intended to soften the architectural lines over time: "Few
shrubs or small plants are indicated and a minimum amount of planted area is called for. Trees, hedges and permanent outdoor structures
are the principal elements added to the site."[61] The short tenure in
Washington also provided him the opportunity to design a garden
for the Gutheims' Georgetown home.

The preliminary design for the Gutheim townhouse garden is dated
10 October 1938 [figure 26]; it could be taken as a collage of the
attitudes and motifs proffered in the Small Gardens project.[62] The
plan of the long narrow lot was developed along a path that alternated between a flowing biomorphic line and the zigzag borrowed
from Pierre-Émile Legrain. Terrace and stair connected the second
floor directly to the garden, enclosing a sunken court to the north of
the house, cool in summer. The movement from interior to the raised
*giardino segreto* centered on an existing catalpa at the opposite end
of the site. The presence of the hidden garden was revealed by a
small pool animated by a jet, a structure for tea roses, a perennial

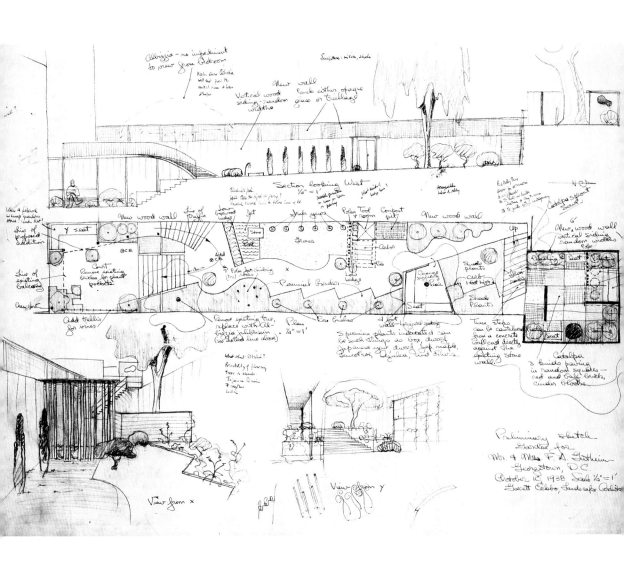

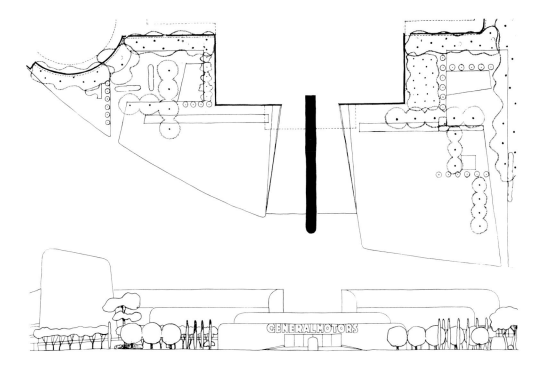

**25**
Ludwig Mies van der Rohe.
German Pavilion [recon-
struction]. Interior view
looking toward court.
Barcelona, Spain, 1929.
[*Marc Treib*]

**26**
Gutheim garden.
Preliminary plan.
Georgetown, Washington,
D.C., 1938.
Pencil on tracing paper.
[*Documents Collection*]

**27**
General Motors Pavilion,
New York World's Fair.
Study for the landscape
design, 1938. Photostat.
[*Documents Collection*]

border, Irish yews, and a host of other more architectural features such as seats and an arbor. The design was far more complex than its site demanded — or even comfortably allowed. It demonstrated how restlessly Eckbo was chafing at the bit, raring to apply as many of his recently developed modernist garden ideas to whatever commission came his way. But he would have to wait; the scheme was realized only in part.

For a short time thereafter, again through Gutheim's auspices, Eckbo worked in the office of Norman Bel Geddes. His assignment there was the landscape design for the General Motors Pavilion for the 1939 New York World's Fair, in particular, the area surrounding the building's principal facade [figure 27]. Modeling the ground plane as a series of earthen terraces and using tree plantings to articulate a series of green zones, Eckbo attempted to complement the building's streamlined masses in landscape form. For Eckbo, this was time to play and explore — in theory, Bel Geddes was interested in advanced landscape ideas to match the architecture of the pavilion. But the final scheme, the one witnessed in photographs of the fair, focused on the procession of visitors who wound their way up the ramps on the pavilion's flank. Little vegetation was used; the reality of the pavilion was the exhibit within.[63] In the end, the Eckbo landscape proposals had come to naught, except to provide the young landscape architect and his wife with sufficient funds to return to California. They did so at the end of 1938.

**Return of the Prodigal**

"Why don't you go on west to California?" said the "owner men" in John Steinbeck's *Grapes of Wrath:* "There's work there and it never gets cold. Why, you can reach out anywhere and pick an orange. Why there's always some kind of crop to work in. Why don't you go there?"[64]

Like the Joad family, Garrett Eckbo was lured back to California not only by nostalgia but also by the promise of a job — in the Farm Security Administration (FSA) office in San Francisco. When Eckbo arrived late in 1938, however, the position had evaporated. He sought work from Thomas Church and was taken on immediately. Their association as employer and employee did not last long — two weeks to be exact. At that time, the FSA job rose again with the promise of slightly greater pay. Eckbo asked Church to match the FSA offer; Church declined, and Eckbo entered the ranks of government functionaries. Filled with advanced landscape design ideas, social ideals, and a considerable population of migrant farmworkers for which to design, the recent graduate joined a talented team of designers working in the FSA's western office.[65]

Regionalism, with the reexamination of the locale, was a theme underlying many New Deal programs, from the Federal Writer's Project to local art programs. Regionalism asserted the knowledge and experience of a particular place over a broader idea of the nation as a whole, expressing "the need for a sense of place amid the stress and dislocation of the depression." For an agricultural society in turmoil, with hundreds of thousands of displaced nomads forced to wander on western roads, the idea of soil, roots, and home became a preoccupation. "This land, this red land, is us," wrote John Steinbeck, "and the flood years and the dust years and the drought years are us." In the flight that followed dispossession, farmers dreamed of the land from which they had been driven: "How'll it be not to know what land's outside the door? How if you wake up in the night and know — and know the willow tree's not there? Can you live without the willow tree? Well no, you can't."[66]

The regard for things regional exerted an essentially conservative — in its literal sense — influence upon art and design, denying continental avant-garde imports for themes validating what were believed to be distinctively American concepts. The reconstruction of Williamsburg, the elevation of Mt. Vernon to the status of shrine, and the FSA photographic project reveal common origins in the search for heritage. It was an urge that also found expressions in landscape design and buildings that evoked the perceived stability of prior eras, such as the structures based on local historical prototypes built by the National Park Service.

Throughout the country, projects for parks and recreational facilities, rose gardens and campgrounds challenged landscape designers to maximize the impact of minimal means and the often unskilled labor force of the Civilian Conservation Corps. The designs tended to reflect regional themes grounded in sentiment. *Park and Recreation*

*Structures*, a three-volume handbook written by Albert H. Good and published by the National Park Service in 1938, represented the best of local and federal governmental sponsored work, from signing and water fountains to lodges and trailer camps. It became the standard reference work for decades. In the foreword to the first volume Arno Cammerer, director of the National Park Service, established the prerogatives for park design:

> A basic objective of those who are entrusted with development of such areas [modifications of the natural landscape] for human uses for which they are established is, it seems to me, to hold these modifications to a minimum and so design them that, besides being attractive to look upon, they appear to belong to and be a part of their settings.[67]

Although this statement could be interpreted and utilized by an architect such as Frank Lloyd Wright to produce Taliesin West, for the most part the illustrations and message of the books argued for a traditional expression drawing upon indigenous architecture and materials. "More than any other regional issue," wrote Michael Steiner, "sense of place offered a promise of order, security and self-understanding."[68] Eckbo never denied the importance of these longings, but he did not readily accept the assumed prescription of a regional or traditional expression for them so common to the National Park Service.

**28**

Park and community building. Harlingen, Texas, 1940. Farm Security Administration.

Ink on tracing paper.

[Documents Collection]

Among its assignments, the western office of the Farm Security Administration was charged with providing minimal living conditions for agricultural workers, both migrant and more sedentary, focused on California, Arizona, and Texas. To meet the constantly increasing demands for housing, the authority's designers created a series of camps, many of them in California's Central Valley, that used almost every available form of housing stock. The solutions ranged from tents to trailers to metal sheds; none of them fancy, all of them minimal. These were all standardized units — despised by the program's architects — and the contributions of the FSA designers were primarily in the planning of the communities and in the humanization of exterior spaces against the harsh climates of the arid land.

Eckbo worked on the design of almost fifty camps during his four-odd

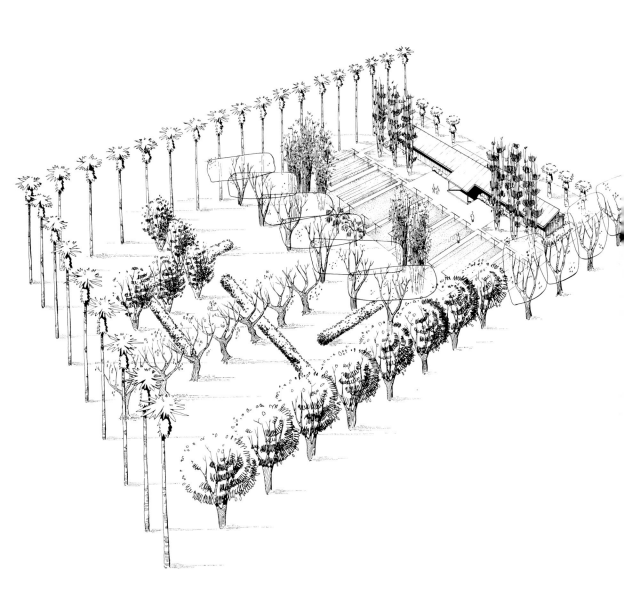

years with the administration, relying on a relatively stable approach to layout and landscape. While many projects, such as the Taft or Shafter camps, used a hexagonal or modified hexagonal arrangement, some schemes were less formal and developed more directly from local site conditions. The designers planned an architectural ecology of sorts, in which platform tents or trailers would be succeeded by more permanent metal housing, probably of little actual improvement given its poor insulative qualities. Finally, apartment blocks or detached houses might be built [see plate II].

In these projects, as in most of his community landscape designs, rows of trees or hedges reduced the velocity of winds and provided shade; their linear alignments or sinuous curves unified the spaces surrounding individual structures, in effect creating a landscape superstructure to which the minimal buildings were subservient. Plant lists were surprisingly varied, with most of the trees brought to the site, others transplanted within the same site or from other proximate FSA projects. These included cottonwood, Chinese elm, sycamore, mulberry, and other hardy species.

The highlights of the landscape schemes were the park or community areas in which the group spaces of laundry structures, meeting rooms, or playgrounds were extended outward [figure 28]. In *Landscape for Living*, Eckbo presented twelve variants for the same park space for the camp near Weslaco, Texas, demonstrating how to create genetically affiliated spatial designs using a simplified — yet consistent — vocabulary [see figures 98, 99]. All these areas were intended to be irrigated and kept green. Water resources were usually available because the camps occupied sites previously used as farms or ranches. In some instances, the grand ideas — both social and vegetal — languished with lack of maintenance. Dorothea Lange's photographic documentation made the limits of the FSA's interventions only too clear, discussed by Dorothée Imbert in the following essay.[69]

In retrospect, the success of the FSA projects might be qualified, but rarely the idealism of their enterprise. Housing by Burton Cairns and Vernon DeMars at Chandler, Arizona, and Yuba City were among the earliest social housing in the United States, cited and published widely. The landscape ideas that complemented these projects — led by Garrett Eckbo and his classmates Corwin Mocine and Francis Violich — matched in energy and zeitgeist the most advanced of architectural ideas. In almost all of these landscape designs, the spatial ideas found in Modernist architectural space were applied to desiccated landscapes or agricultural fields. Versions of Eckbo's Contempoville were realized up and down the length of California, reduced to an almost pathetic level of means, but with no reduction in the intensity of their spatial investigation or humanity.

During his employment with the FSA, Eckbo moonlighted on private commissions and took an active part in the discussion of relevant professional and social issues. Telesis, an informal alliance of design practitioners based in San Francisco, was formed to address the problems facing the environment of the Bay Area. The first meeting was held in the Eckbo house on Telegraph Hill in 1939, with a core group that included architects Burton Cairns, Vernon DeMars, and Phillip Joseph; planner T. J. Kent; landscape architects Francis Violich and Corwin Mocine (who would become planners); and industrial designer Walter Landor, among others. In July 1940 the group held an exhibition at the San Francisco Museum of Art, arguing for comprehensive planning, the joining of social, political, and physical planning concerns, and an integration of the design professions in outlook and collaboration. Although Eckbo served as editor of a West Coast issue of *Task* in late 1944, the group's cohesion — if not its idealism — had been seriously undermined by the demands of war, at home and in battle.[70]

With the American entry into World War II, the FSA agency turned its attention to defense workers' housing for their constantly growing numbers in the San Francisco Bay Area and central California. Of the existing government agencies, only the FSA held a positive track record for producing housing and community facilities, on time and more or less on budget: "Neither [the United States Housing Authority nor the Public Buildings Administration] was very effective, and by the spring of 1941 the housing program was the furthest behind schedule of all defense building efforts."[71] The result was the FSA's undertaking of defense workers' housing and the formation of the Division of Defense Housing to meet the ever-growing population surges into California.

## The War Years, The Postwar Years

The lingering effects of a 1939 auto accident, in which Burton Cairns was killed, kept Eckbo from active military service.[72] And a few weeks' work in a Sausalito shipyard convinced Eckbo that his talent lay in design; he went to work for the war effort, planning four dozen schemes within a three-year period. The site and landscape development for the community and commercial center in Vallejo, designed by Theodore Bernardi and Ernest Kump, paralleled designs by Thomas Church for housing by William Wurster on other parts of the site. The means were meager; the allotted time, virtually none. Once again, sinuous lines of poplars doubled as spatial integrators and windbreaks, softening the relentless march of standardized units that followed the contours of the grassy hillsides.

With hostilities ended in August 1945, America began the return to normalcy. Given the transplanted minions of workers who elected to remain in the Golden State, the GI Bill that gave veterans access to education and homes, and the basic optimism that accompanied the nonmartial economy, California boomed. Suburbs developed on the perimeter of every major city in the state, soon to be rendered the inside of the city and not its edge.[73] Freeways provided access to greater and greater amounts of land gobbled by suburban development, calling for more freeways and even greater development. The cycle never abated.

Eckbo formed a partnership with his brother-in-law, Edward Williams, in 1940 and designed a number of gardens in the San Francisco Bay Area while employed with the FSA and war housing programs.[74] At a Telesis gathering before the war, Eckbo met Robert Royston, who worked for Thomas Church from the late 1930s until he entered military service. Royston, always known as an extremely talented designer, became a mainstay of the Church office and supervised the defense workers' housing project in Vallejo. By mail, Eckbo invited him to join the firm as partner upon his release from the Navy, where he was serving in the Pacific theater. Royston had come within a hairsbreadth of partnership with Church: "When I got home Tommy had my name on the door. It was a difficult period for me because I liked Tommy very much and we had a close relationship. But Garrett always attracted me because he's a clear and social thinker, and he can really see the whole picture." He described practice as a brand-new world where "we could experiment right and left."[75]

Eckbo, Royston and Williams was established in 1945, and within five years it had become one of the leading firms in the country, highly regarded for its advanced planning ideas, innovative modern vocabulary, and its quality of execution. It was during these years that the distinctive Eckbo idiom developed, prompted by the association with Robert Royston, and in collaboration with leading architects such as Joseph Stein, John Funk, and John Dinwiddie. To some degree, these designs developed ideas first proposed in the Small Gardens and Contempoville studies, but each of these ideas was tempered by the particular conditions of the site and program.

The 1939 garden for Mr. and Mrs. F. M. Fisk in Atherton had allowed Eckbo to work at larger residential scale, pairing sunny lawn and "natural meadow" areas with layered spaces defined by hedges, set under oaks and redwoods [figures 29, 30]. The net effect was one of openness and enclosure, sun and shade, boundary and vista. That no aspect of the garden was perceived as absolute is also suggested in a pencil study for the Reid garden in Palo Alto from the same period [figure 31]. The low hedges established an orthogonal structure in which the house reverberated in the garden; but the overarching frame of trees led the eye over and beyond these spatial dividers toward the horizon. For John Dinwiddie's 1941 Frazier Cole house in Oakland, Eckbo used curving planes of wooden screen walls to enclose fluid spaces around the house, protecting them from unwanted street noise and outside view [figures 32, 33].

As a group, the designs for northern California gardens of the period following immediately after the war could best be characterized as considerate of their clients' needs and the dicta of the site, and intelligent in deriving forms to suite those requirements. Although touches of modernity appear in their spatial definition, in the curving of a wall or in the use of some offbeat paving material, the gardens

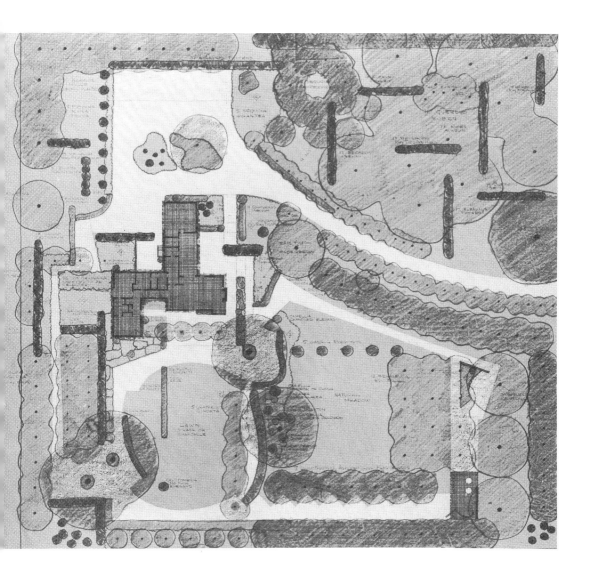

**29**
Fisk garden. Site plan.
Atherton, 1939.
Photostat.
[*Courtesy Garrett Eckbo*]

**30**
Fisk garden.
View southwest over the
lawn area.
Atherton, 1939.
[*Courtesy Garrett Eckbo*]

**31**
Reid garden. Study.
Palo Alto, circa 1940.
Photostat.

[*Courtesy Garrett Eckbo*]

**33**
Cole garden. Retaining wall
with built-in barbecue —
and Garrett Eckbo.
Oakland, 1941. Photostat.
[*Philip Fein, courtesy Garrett
Eckbo*]

**32**
Cole garden.
Axonometric view.
Oakland, 1941.
Photostat.
[*Courtesy Garrett Eckbo*]

remained polite and restrained, lacking the full-blown exuberance of the following years in southern California.

Each partner ran his own projects, and interests and formal vocabularies varied to some degree from their common sensibility. A profile of the year-old firm, "A Professional Adventure in Use of Outdoor Space," appeared in the September 1946 issue of *Architect and Engineer*. It not only illustrated the gathering esteem with which Eckbo, Royston and Williams' production was held by the professional community, but also the qualities the partners held in common:

> Their principle of work is: Work — *They like their work and like to work.* Provide the best possible service — *They believe in thoroughness, attention to detail, and recognize that quantity without quality is nothing.* Get recognition for good work — *They don't believe in hiding their light under a bushel. They feel very seriously that unless they produce the best quality work that they will not have a place in the profession.*[76]

Eckbo and Royston appear to have been the stronger landscape designers; Williams gravitated toward projects of larger scale, such as recreation and community planning. At this time, Royston's garden designs tended to favor a vivid play of curved and angular planes defining the "open center," usually a lawn or paved patio. The garden or park's central space predominated, supported by secondary areas formed with fences, hedges, and trees [figures 34, 35].

For landscape architects, the housing boom provided almost unlimited opportunities, especially in the Southland. The evolving California pattern of indoor-outdoor living required designed exterior space to complement interior subdivisions. The Case Study House program, sponsored by *Arts and Architecture* magazine between 1948 and 1962, realized demonstration projects that included gardens as a vital part of the design. Eckbo's landscape designs accompanied projects by Rodney Walker in Beverly Hills from 1947 and Conrad Buff, Calvin Straub, and Donald Hensman's 1958 Case Study House #20 in Altadena. These designs for display were necessarily less assertive than gardens designed for specific clients but they provided the perfect accompaniments — and counterpoints — to the architecture of their respective houses [figure 36].[77]

**34**
Robert Royston.
Platt garden.
Axonometric view.
Oakland, circa 1946.
[*from* Architect and Engineer]

**35**
Robert Royston.
The Palo Alto. Pool area.
Palo Alto, 1950s.
[*Louis Alley, courtesy Robert Royston*]

## The Move South

Eckbo held fond memories of the Southland from his short tenure with
Armstrong Nurseries in the mid-1930s, and saw the vast sea of
opportunities for landscape architects there. In contrast to the more
restrained design arena of northern California, the Los Angeles area
had been open to the aesthetic avant-garde since the 1920s. For
Eckbo: "There was a sense of drive, action, dynamism that I had never
felt in the north." This innovative climate, perhaps spurred on by the
film industry, had fostered unbridled experiments in space and form,
from the early houses of architects including Frank Lloyd Wright, R. M.
Schindler, and Richard Neutra, to the Second Generation represented by John Lautner, Gregory Ain, Craig Ellwood, and Raphael Soriano,
among others.[78] The influx of émigrés beginning in the 1930s further
stimulated developments in art (Marcel Duchamp and Salvador Dalí),
music (Arnold Schoenberg), film (several Austrian directors including
Josef von Sternberg, Fritz Lang, and Billy Wilder), and literature
(Thomas Mann). Eckbo scrutinized both the artistic possibilities in the
Los Angeles area and its burgeoning economy and population —
which translated into extensive building opportunities. From 1945
on, he began to spend one week a month in Los Angeles: beating the
bushes for work and keeping an eye on the projects on the boards
and in the ground. For a roof, he used a spare room in the house of
Gregory Ain, who would become a fast friend and frequent collaborator. By the end of the year he had secured sufficient work to open
the office.

Thus, in late 1946, Garrett and Arline Eckbo moved south; a southern branch of Eckbo, Royston and Williams was opened, renting
space for two years from the architect Robert Alexander in the
Baldwin Hills Village Golf Club. From the beginning, each office and
partner was relatively independent, with quarterly meetings for
review and planning. "Mutual respect and cooperation were exem-
plary," Eckbo remembers. Because of the tight housing market, the
Eckbos first rented an apartment in San Pedro, south of the city, but
in time found a house more centrally located.[79] Los Angeles was
booming, architecture was thriving, and the desire for outdoor living
— before the widespread use of air conditioning — was reaching its
apogee [figure 37; see plate IX]. The potent combination of peace,

**36**
Case Study House #20.
Pool area with Italian stone
pine. Altadena, 1958.
Buff, Straub and Hensman,
architects.
[*Julius Shulman, courtesy
Garrett Eckbo*]

growing prosperity, the relaxation of building material restrictions, and the psychological release from years of austerity — all tinged with personal aggrandizement — made the garden a desirable commodity. The practice flourished, producing garden after garden for clients with existing houses, or in conjunction with housing built to the designs of modernist architects.

In gardens that can be counted in the high hundreds, if not the thousands, Eckbo investigated and reinvestigated the play among space, activity, geometry, climate, and vegetation. The garden's dynamic or more lyrical composition countered the more stolid form of the house and its orthogonal relation to the lot lines [figure 38]. Eckbo "understood that the modern garden had fewer constraints than the modern house, which was concerned with function, efficiency and economy," wrote the landscape architect and professor Michael Laurie. "The garden could be approached much as a sculptor approaches a new block of stone or as a painter, brush in hand, stands before a blank canvas" [figure 39]. The architectonic framework of the garden — commonly built for purposes of physical enclosure or visual screening — structured zones of use and aesthetic space. Vegetation at first played only a secondary role, but in time planting achieved greater prominence [figure 40].[80] Thus, within a handful of years after the war, the elements of Eckbo's mature style were already apparent: staggered, interlocking spaces articulated by a mixture of angled walls, often terminated by a circular space defined by an arcing wall or curving row of trees.

## Picture Space, Landscape Space

The source of these formal manipulations lay, once again, in modern art. While the landscape architect rarely mentions specific influences, the Eckbo gardens of the late 1940s and 1950s, are so close to certain works by Wassily Kandinsky as to beg comparison. In his quest for the "spiritual in art," Kandinsky examined the relationships among nonobjective elements within the space of the picture. Like his contemporary and Bauhaus colleague Paul Klee, Kandinsky often relied on primary visual signifiers such as lines, dots, circles, and planes to create compositions with metaphysical aspirations. He believed that "the more abstract is form, the more clear and direct its appeal." Yet he

**37**
Kiernan garden.
Los Angeles, mid-1950s.
The openness of the
house extends into the
sunny areas — grassed or
paved — with trees and a
lath house providing shade.
[*John Hartley, courtesy
Garrett Eckbo*]

**38**
Goldin garden.
Laurel Canyon,
Los Angeles, mid-1950s.
Distinctly shaped areas of
paving, and an irrigated and
manicured lawn, contrast
significantly with the natural
landscape beyond.
[*Courtesy Garrett Eckbo*]

admitted that the average person "does not probe the outer expression to arrive at inner meaning" — as one should.[81] The strong V composition created by two powerful diagonal lines locks the circle between them; arcs reinforce the position of the circle, but only indirectly. Alfred Barr published Kandinsky's *Composition 1* (1921) [see figure 19] in *Cubism and Abstract Art,* a publication with which Eckbo was familiar even during his Harvard years.

For Kandinsky, the idea of composition comprised both the work as a whole and the "various forms, [which] by standing in different relationships to each other, decide the composition of the whole.... Singly they will have little meaning, being of importance only in so far as they help the general effect." But as a group, "they have to serve as the building material for the whole composition."[82] In all, the construction is simultaneously anchored and yet dynamic, appearing predominantly two-dimensional, yet opening to a spatial reading in which the nonobjective shapes are held in dynamic suspension.

Diverse sources inspired Kandinsky's paintings and led to his triad of types: impressions, improvisations, and compositions. Indicatively, Kandinsky stated that "reason, consciousness, purpose" played a central role in the series termed "compositions." *Composition VIII* (1923) developed from a far denser concentration of lines, dots, and triangles, and yet the linear wedge and circle remained predominant [figure 41]. In his *Pedagogical Sketchbook,* Paul Klee postulated "a harmonization of elements toward an independent, calm-dynamic, and dynamic-calm entity. This composition can only be complete if movement is met by counter-movement or if a solution of kinetic infinity has been found."[83] The goal was to cast dynamic elements in dynamic equilibrium. In certain respects, Eckbo seemed to share this intention, modified in its application to spatial design.

It is Kandinsky's compositions that constitute the closest parallels to Eckbo's southern California works of the late 1940s and 1950s. Like them, Eckbo's mature gardens relied on circles as termini or places of stasis, defined by benches, lawn, or the white line of a concrete mowing strip. The most exuberant of these designs was the unrealized 1945 landscape design for the estate of Mr. and Mrs. William Burden in Westchester County, New York [figure 42]. The architects for the house were Harrison & Abramowitz, and Eckbo credits Isamu

**39**
Eggers garden.
Axonometric view.
Pasadena, 1946.
Ink on tracing paper.
The garden's fragmented
or curving profiles contrast
with the orthogonal box of
the house — shown here
only in outline.
[*Documents Collection*]

**40**
Shulman garden.
Nighttime view.
Laurel Canyon, Los
Angeles, 1950.
Raphael Soriano, architect.
[*Julius Shulman*]

**41**

Wassily Kandinsky,
*Composition VIII*, 1923.

*[David Heald, © Solomon R.*
*Guggenheim Foundation,*
*New York]*

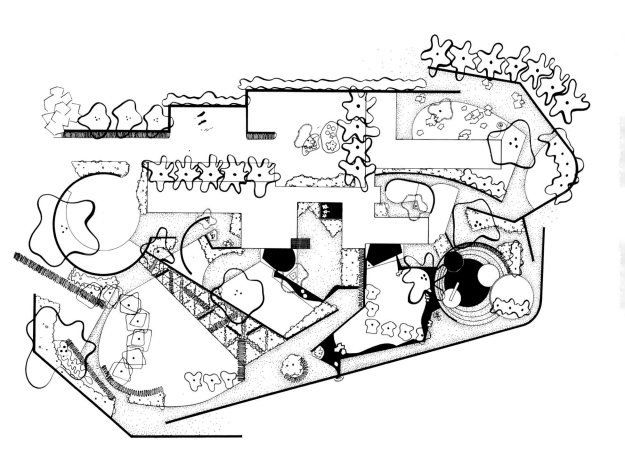

**42**
Burden garden. Plan.
Westchester County,
New York, 1945.
Harrison & Abramowitz,
architects.
Ink on tracing paper.
[*Documents Collection*]

Noguchi as sculptor on the project, although his contribution is unspecified. The scheme was vintage Eckbo: a circular swimming pool enclosure complemented the circular opening in the roof; flower beds slashed diagonally across the site, linking a second circular court to the garden proper. The garden became a world of spatial fragments and planted set as particles within a chemical suspension — there is a sense of the whole, although each part remains identifiable, true also of several others projects from this period [figure 43].[84]

Certain aspects of László Moholy-Nagy's works also resonated in Eckbo's gardens of the late 1940s and early 1950s. In several series of prints, the artist used packages of skewed lines to energize the surface of the works [figure 44]. In the project for two adjacent houses, Eckbo used wooden strips set obliquely in the concrete terrace to expand outward the sensed limits of the house [figure 45].

Klee described the circle as the trace of the pendulum, suggesting a development in time.[85] The plan for the unexecuted 1944 Nickel garden in California's Central Valley played a circular lawn against the house's L-shaped plan [figure 46]. From this central living area in stasis, the garden dramatically expanded, a powerfully centrifugal design that integrated within its radiating geometry the children's play areas, a polite zone of lawn and shade, and the pasture that allows cattle to become a part of the activities. The auto court was positioned on the far side of the house, isolated from the central garden, set within a zone assigned to vegetables, court games, and swimming. The circle was most clearly witnessed in plan, but a more careful reading of the design reveals that the garden was to be composed of angular segments arranged within a circular superstructure — there was little except the heart of the scheme that could ever be perceived as a circle. The insistence of the geometry gave way to the use of the garden's areas, defined — in Eckbo's now-signature manner using lower hedges and wooden fences and higher, more insistent curving planes of trees.

**43**

Bay Lido Building.
Pocket park.
Newport Beach, 1958.

[*Julius Shulman*]

In its use of a pure, circular organization, the Nickel garden was quite rare. The site's confines pressured the circle of the Firk garden in Los Angeles [preliminary plan 1952] into an irregular oval, the pergola and other walls pushed to the patio's perimeter [see plate VII]. More

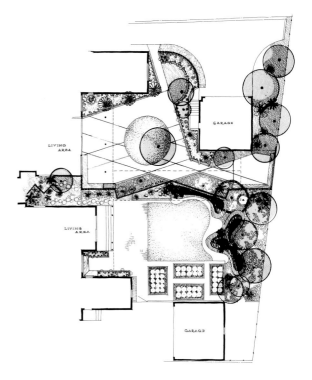

**44**
László Moholy-Nagy.
*AXL II*, 1927.
[*David Heald*, © *Solomon R. Guggenheim Foundation*]

---

**45**
Garden project for two neighbors.
Los Angeles, mid-1950s.
Ink on tracing paper.
Convolution of the property line wall extended the sense of limit in each garden.
[*Courtesy Garrett Eckbo*]

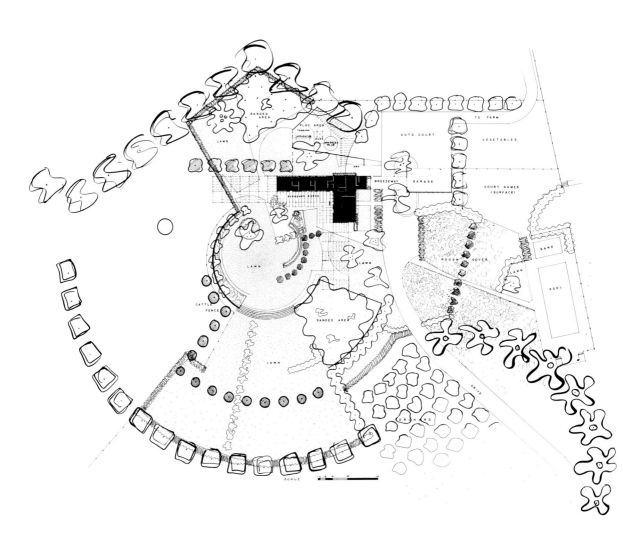

SANDED
AREA

LAWN

PLAY AREA
APPARATUS

TO FARM

AUTO COURT

VEGETABLES

DRY

BREEZEWAY    GARAGE

COURT GAMES
(SURFACE)

LAWN

ROUGH   COVER

SAND

LAWN

LAWN

CATTLE
FENCE

SANDED AREA

LAWN

POOL

DRIVE

ORCHARD

SCALE

commonly, in Eckbo's compositional strategy, the circle anchored the dynamic thrust of the diagonal line and was rarely left undefiled. Instead, elements such as a planting bed or pool on the ground, or trellises or roof planes above, overlapped the circular perimeter. Like the painter's use of elements such as the point, the line, and the plane, the landscape architect used the usual elements of path, hedge, singular plant, paving materials, water, wall, and trellis. Although these were reformed by a modern vocabulary, it was less the redefinition of any singular element (except perhaps the shape of the pool or planting bed) than the correlation of planes and forms in space that distinguished Eckbo's compositions.

The 1959 design for the Sudarsky garden in Bakersfield summarized both the social and formal aspects of Eckbo's manner, combined to effect a modern landscape for living [figures 47, 48]. Since the house faced north, the auto court occupied the southern part of the site, the preferred exposure for the garden. As a result, Eckbo positioned the principal outdoor living areas to the west. The circle appeared modified as a stellate entrance feature, as a smaller northern patio with ornamental pool, as the basis of a recreational lawn area, and as a cusp enclosing the swimming pool. The various zones of activity merged, however, undermining the rigidity of the geometrical shape, as did the preponderance of ornamental planting.

After the landscape architect's removal to Los Angeles, Gregory Ain and Eckbo had become frequent collaborators. Many of their projects concerned multi-family developments and apartments in addition to single-family houses. With Ain, Eckbo furthered his ideas on the relation of the community to the land and the relation of the house to the community, stressing that "the front yard is the direct physical connection between the private home and its neighborhood." His personal social contract addressed the role of the individual in society, and that role as expressed in the built environment:

> Thus the relations between each private home and its neighborhood involve continuous choices between social and private living, sociability and privacy, community services and self-sufficient labor, what portions of life can best be handled individually and what portions can best be handled through some form of cooperation within the community.

**46**
Nickel garden. Site plan.
Los Banos, 1944.
Mario Corbett, architect.
Ink on tracing paper.
[*Documents Collection*]

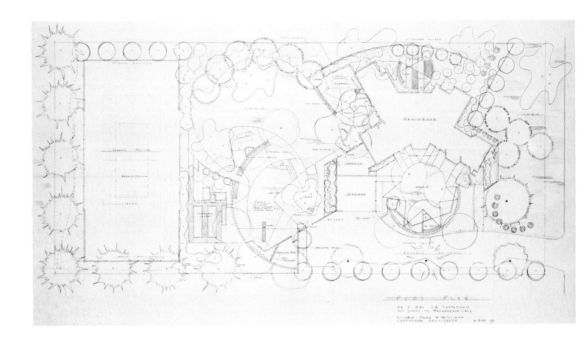

**47**
Sudarsky garden.
Site Plan. Bakersfield, 1959.
Pencil on tracing paper.

[*Documents Collection*]

**48**
Sudarsky garden.
View over swimming pool,
looking east.
Bakersfield, 1959.

[*George Reineking, courtesy
Garrett Eckbo*]

Various projects, discussed in the following essay, demonstrated Eckbo and company's test developments for the several cooperative groups. On flat sites, the layouts were often unabashedly geometric, with alignments of tree planting used to provide the spatial superstructure that links individual dwellings. "The over-all pattern of trees in a neighborhood of detached houses," Eckbo wrote, "is the single most important visual element."[86] His regard for this precept is apparent even today in the 1948 Modernique homes in the Mar Vista district of Los Angeles [see figures 124–28; plate III]. Here, plantings of magnolia, melaleuca, and ficus prevail, offering a homogenous canopy for houses that have taken various guises through remodeling over the year. Landscape design continues the neighborhood as that point where the limit of the individual house and site ceases. Landscape architecture thus integrates the suburban community almost as the wall creates contiguous urbanity [figures 49a–c, 50].

For individual clients, the process was often the reverse, seeking to create a domestic paradise within the tight limits of the suburban lot. The intention was to maximize the potentials of the given area and to magnify the sense of space, once the conditions of the program had been met. If the front lawn, with its "structural" use of trees, was intended as a link between adjacent properties, then the design of the rear yard or garden tried to eradicate the insistence of neighboring houses and unwanted views [figures 51, 52, 53]. Given the tight confines of many of these sites, the living zones of the gardens were forced to overlap, almost always spatially, and often in terms of function [see plate VIII]. Only rarely was there a singular grand vista: a motif such as the zigzag itself prompted movement and the revelation of views through time. Although his garden designs tended to be internally oriented, within their own world, they also magnified the possibilities within their limits. Of course, the design depended on whether or not the site was bounded or open. But unlike Thomas Church, whose garden designs tended to lead the eye outward, capturing the surroundings as a part of the composition, the constrictions of many Eckbo gardens made masking logical and an internal focus necessary. The designs set the scene for outdoor living — which included increasingly popular swimming pools for those who could afford them — and choreographed movement and vistas internally and externally.

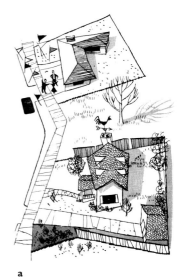

a

**49a–c**
As illustrated in this sketch, and on succeeding right hand pages, Eckbo advocated the development of the suburban landscape through judicious planning. Carlos Diniz, delineator.
[*from Garrett Eckbo, The Art of Home Landscaping*]

**50**

Taub garden. Entrance
court looking north.
Los Angeles, 1957.

[*Courtesy Garrett Eckbo*]

**51**

Koolish garden.
Fountain court.
Bel Air, 1952.

[*Julius Shulman*]

**52**

Harryman garden.
Los Angeles, mid-1950s.
Banked earth, reinforced by
plantings, screened
unwanted views.

[*Courtesy Garrett Eckbo*]

## The Pool in the Garden

In 1941 Margaret Olthof Goldsmith advised her presumably affluent clients that "When you think of the money spent in renting a summer cottage on a distant lake or seaside, and in getting there year after year, you will find a swimming pool a good investment.… No one who has a good swimming pool will deny that it yields a return that justifies its cost." Despite this sheaf of purported benefits, she admitted that "it is costly, just as an automobile is costly." The incidence of swimming pool construction in southern California continued to mount after the war, while the price of pools continued to drop. Even in far-off New York State, presumably the setting for John Cheever's "The Swimmer," the pool had become such a ubiquitous element of the domestic landscape that the story's protagonist could consider swimming across a sequence of suburban backyards: "He seemed to see, with a cartographer's eye, that string of swimming pools, that quasi-subterranean stream that curved across the county."[87] Given that Los Angeles is essentially an irrigated desert, the swimming pool became an object of intense desire for those with the means to build them [see plate IX].

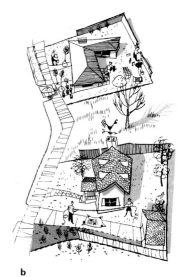

b

Its dimensions often made a pool the garden's most prominent feature, and in many of the Eckbo designs it became the point of departure for the spatial composition [figures 54, 55]. Given its aristocratic birth in the estates of the wealthy, the pool was normally set off from the principal part of the garden and screened from view. But the restricted lot sizes of Californian suburban development precluded such a privileged distinction, and the landscape architect was forced to integrate the pool into the garden as a central feature. For Thomas Church the pool served a multitude of purposes both aesthetic and useful:

> It can remain a simple reflection pool in the garden, in which you
> occasionally take a dip, or become a complete entertainment
> center where you have as many fascinations for children and
> guests as you can dream up. It may have a cabana with shade
> and lemonade, or maybe it has a bar. If there are youngsters
> around, it might have a soda fountain and a sandwich counter.
> If your guests stay for the weekend, it can double as a guest
> house.[88]

**53**
Chappell garden.
Bel Air, mid-1950s.
Although the redwood
bench demarcated the limit
of the patio, planting
intruded, softening the
sense of boundary.

[*Maynard Parker, courtesy
Garrett Eckbo*]

**54**
Pool and pergolas,
Bellehurst Estates.
Los Angeles, late 1950s.

[*Julius Shulman*]

**55**
Reiner garden.
Los Angeles, late 1956.
John Lautner, architect.
The waterline extends to
the very edge of the pool,
visually merging with the
Silver Lake reservoir
beyond.

[*Courtesy Garrett Eckbo*]

Thomas Church's Donnell garden of 1948 immortalized the kidney as the archetypical Californian pool shape.[89] With its command of a hilltop in Sonoma County, its sweeping view toward San Francisco Bay, and the contemporary flavor of its swimming pool, the design captured the imagination of readers and designers, nationally and internationally, as the epitome of a modern setting for outdoor living [figure 56]. But if the pool's shape could embody absolute contemporaneity in some Church designs, it could also play a more refined role, almost in the manner of a classical Italian garden. Church's Henderson garden in Hillsborough from 1958, for example, used the pool to establish the axis of the central area, linking the house with the landscape beyond [figure 57].

Eckbo, in contrast, found in water a more active catalyst for reading the space, using to advantage both the pool's exotic shape and its relation to other elements of the garden composition [figures 58-60; see plates X, XI, XVI]. Writing to the professional, he suggested the place of the liquid in the garden design:

> The landscape architect must think of water, not only as a provider of coolness and repose or motion or life, or even as a translucent veil which intensifies the color and texture of any material across which it is drawn, but also (because one does not step into a pool without careful preparation) as a positive space-organizing element which controls physical movement, knocking a hole in the site, but does not block the movement of the eye.[90]

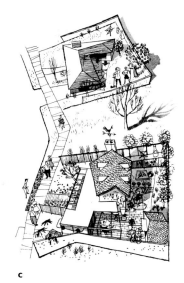

c

Thus water—most notably as swimming pools—came to prominence in Eckbo's postwar garden designs for the arid Southland.

Pool form varied with the shape of the site, orientation, location, and its compositional function within the garden. Put simply, "the garden must shape the pool, rather than being forced to conform to it." One pool, for example, anchored a garden design intended to expand "the outlook direction derived from the house form."[91] To accommodate a paraplegic client, for whom water offered pleasure as well as exercise, a pool was bent and gently sloped for wheelchair access [figure 61; see plate XI]. In contrast, to maximize the dramatic potential of the pool for a bathing suit designer, the Cole garden in Beverly Hills

**56**
Thomas Church.
Donnell garden.
Pool with sculpture by
Adaline Kent.
Sonoma County, 1948.
[*Marc Treib*]

**57**
Thomas Church.
Henderson garden.
Hillsborough, 1958.
William Wurster, architect.
[*Marc Treib*]

**58**
Hartman garden.
Axonometric view of pool
and pool house.
Beverly Hills, 1946.
Pencil on tracing paper.
[*Documents Collection*]

**59**
Hartman garden.
Beverly Hills, 1946.
[*Julius Shulman*]

**60**
Hartman garden.
Trellis and textured
wooden screen walls.
Beverly Hills, 1946.
[*Julius Shulman*]

concealed a rear pool area from view. Models, clad in the latest aquatic fashion, would clandestinely enter and emerge into the main pool from beneath the masonry screen wall [figure 62; see plate X]. Pool shapes ranged from simple rectangles to angular boomerangs, stiff amoebas, and folded kidneys [figure 63]. The formal/spatial idiom might be termed cubo-biomorphic, or simply cubo-bio, an astute mixture of cubistic (or suprematist) forms with the curvilinear shapes that recalled the work of Joan Miró, Jean Arp, or Isamu Noguchi — artists with whom Eckbo was well acquainted.[92]

Of the hundreds of gardens designed by Eckbo during the period from 1946 to 1960, the Goldstone garden in Beverly Hills serves as a typical, if extreme, example. The sweeping arched wall of the garden, completed in 1948, confronted the living spaces of the existing house [figures 64, 65]. The forms of the garden are in fact alien to both their site and the style of the architecture; instead, the landscape is a respite from banality, a more perfect world of contemporary form, shape, materials — a sculpture encompassing living outdoors [figures 66, 67]. In plan an active and complicated geometry played angled walls against the swimming pool of composite rectangular/circular profile. These elements were unified by the sweeping masonry and glass bottle wall that backdropped the entire composition. Around 1950 Eckbo became more interested in shade, shadow, pattern, and texture in the garden, as much by architectonic means as by vegetation.[93] The wall reveals those interests. Rather than a conscious decision to use built form instead of plants, the shift seems to have broadened the means for making the garden.

## The Living Garden

In 1949 Eckbo wrote: "We must think of plants as an endlessly varying series of living units, each with its specific cultural requirements, and each with its specific qualities resulting from size, rate of growth, silhouette, structural form, texture, color and fragrance." The new approach reified the role of vegetation in the historical garden, it did not refute it. In current practice, wrote Eckbo in 1948, four reasons for choosing plants prevailed: *practical* planting addressed functional problems such as erosion control; *pictorial* planting offered vegetation as a visual subject; *sentimental* planting "include[d] the rock garden,

**61**
Cranston garden.
Los Angeles, 1950s.
[*Garrett Eckbo*]

**62**
Cole garden.
Beverly Hills, early 1950s.
The masonry wall was supported on a beam spanning the pool, allowing swimmers to emerge from beneath the cantilevered concrete pads.
[*Evans Slater, courtesy Garrett Eckbo*]

**63**
Churchill Apartments.
Patio and pool.
Los Angeles, mid-1950s.
William Lescaze, architect.
[*Courtesy Garrett Eckbo*]

**64**

Goldstone garden. Site plan.
Beverly Hills, 1948.
Once again, the garden's
composition recalls the
work of Kandinsky and
Moholy-Nagy in its free
play of geometric and
soft forms.
Ink on tracing paper.
[*Documents Collection*]

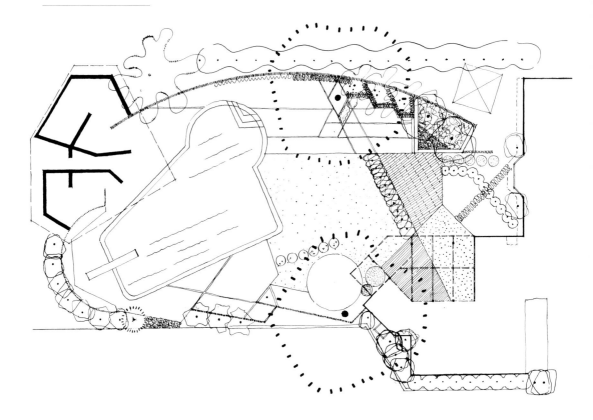

**65**

Goldstone garden.
Beverly Hills, 1948.
The composition joined
pool shape, trellis, and
textured wall — the
existing house served
as foil.
[*Shan Stewart, courtesy
Garrett Eckbo*]

**66**
Goldstone garden.
Bath house.
Beverly Hills, 1948.
[*Julius Shulman*]

**67**

Goldstone garden.
The textured masonry and
bottle wall.
Beverly Hills, 1948.

[*Julius Shulman*]

the old-fashioned garden, bog garden, the English garden—all attempting to recall an emotion." *Commercial* planting, perhaps the most problematic of the four, "tend[ed] to move nursery stock most readily available… without thought to future development or consequences."[94] Today these were untenable, he held, without considering three additional factors: selection, arrangement, and maintenance [figure 68, see plates V, XVII].

Once again, Eckbo balanced his argument using pragmatic with aesthetic factors. "Structural forms follow all variations of symmetry and variety" using their texture, color, and scale to advantage [figure 69]. But *selection* should not be made in isolation, and it is the *arrangement* of plants—their use in combinations—that ultimately governs their success as contributors to the garden. "Most landscape plans start at relating a geometric structure with an irregular site; this requires a concept of form that combines the qualities of more rational geometrical organization with those of nature's free luxuriant growth and continuous development."[95] The final constraint, *maintenance*, colors the reasoning behind selection and arrangement—together, the triad govern the choice of plant species in the contemporary garden.

In several of these gardens the planted areas were reduced in dimensions, using singular trees and vegetation in metal or concrete planters as sculptural forms set against planar backdrops [figure 70]. The sun-catching and thermal-retaining Goldstone garden's wall "of brick, pumice blocks, and bottles, endeavors to extract a maximum expression from the materials by an expanded structuro-sculptural-mural treatment" [figure 67]. This same project also illustrated Eckbo's acknowledging maintenance as a key factor in garden design. For those interested in gardening as a pastime, or for those with sufficient land and means, involved planting schemes were both appropriate and enjoyable. But for those with more limited time, space, funds, and interest, those areas of the garden requiring tending should be kept to a minimum.[96]

Outdoor structures such as pergolas and trellises played an important role in both defining the garden space and accommodating the needs of the family [figure 71]. Occupying a niche between architecture and landscape, these structures, like the shapes of paved areas,

**68**
Rich garden.
Los Angeles, mid-1950s.
[*William Arlin, courtesy
Garrett Eckbo*]

**69**
Webb garden.
Palos Verdes, late 1950s.
The use of planting within
the garden, paired with the
frame created by the
bench, established the
comfortable relationship
between near and far,
inside and out.
[*Julius Shulman*]

**70**
The architectonic frame-
work of the garden
enriched with vegetation.
Carlos Diniz, delineator.
[*from Garrett Eckbo*, The
Art of Home Landscaping]

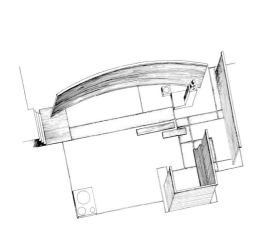

set the tone of the design. For the Goetz garden in Holmby Hills, Eckbo fashioned an overhead trellis that — like the lath house — produced an active pattern of stripes of light and shadow [figure 72]. The metal bents of the pergola become wall and roof simultaneously, railing as well as garden limit [figures 73, 74] — an idea also pursued in the pergola-as-railing of the Edmunds garden in Pacific Palisades.

## A First Book

Amidst the demands of an almost frenetic practice, Eckbo found time to write *Landscape for Living*, published in 1950. It was part an assembly of quotations by others, part recycling of earlier publications, and part an attempt at synthetic thought about the landscape. *Landscape for Living* was Eckbo's almanac and precocious testament that proffered his view of history, his ideas for the present, and his predictions for the future. The book also served to showcase his and Eckbo, Royston and Williams' designs, and he published — as a mix and not always with dates — both student and professional work, projects never intended to be realized and those built.[97]

In the book Eckbo was critical of past thinking, not so much for its role in earlier times, as for the way older landscapes exerted their influence on twentieth-century conditions — conditions, obviously, greatly altered. He believed that the "why" was far more important than the "how," and in fact, was the only ethical basis for contemporary landscape design practice. If we are to produce landscapes for living today, Eckbo argued, we must look far more holistically than garden makers had recourse to, or needed to, in previous eras. Ecology was a major concern, but human beings rightly occupied their position on earth along with other living systems. Nature was not privileged by the author; he was no blind preservationist; instead, he asserted that we must design in accord with nature and create landscapes addressed to contemporary dwelling [figure 75].

While the text does not make for easy reading, and there is no clear structure of greater context to detail, or idea to realization, *Landscape for Living* is as viable today as it was nearly half a century ago. If anything, the ideas have increased in their validity over the passing decades, as the population has grown, technology has become

**71**
Koerner garden.
Palm Springs, late 1950s.
The overhead trellises provided much-needed shade for human and plant alike.
[*Julius Shulman*]

**72**
Goetz garden.
Holmby Hills, 1948.
Trellis materials were used both overhead and in the curving screen wall, creating a dazzling pattern of light and shadow.
[*Courtesy Garrett Eckbo*]

**73**
Goetz garden.
Holmby Hills, 1948.
Edgardo Contini, engineer.
The structure bounding the living area combined a bench, wall, and roof in a single form.
[*Courtesy Garrett Eckbo*]

**74**
Edmunds garden.
Main terrace railing.
Pacific Palisades, 1956.
[*Courtesy Garrett Eckbo*]

more pervasive, and the environment more threatened. We need not support Eckbo's concluding ideas that there should be only two design disciplines, one for creating space, one for objects. But we must take cognizance of his call for a perspective broader than those traditionally held by the individual design professions.

## The Aluminum Garden

If the first section of Garrett Eckbo's career culminated in the public work of the depression and the war years, its second era reached a high point in the Forecast Garden for the Aluminum Company of America (ALCOA). The Wonderland Park development, in which the garden was located, grew from the cooperative plans for the ill-fated Community Homes in Reseda (see following essay). Stymied in the San Fernando Valley by federal loan policies, a number of families regrouped and purchased a tract of land in Laurel Canyon in western Los Angeles.[98] Since the streets had been plotted during an prior attempt at development, Eckbo could provide little comprehensive planning, although he did prepare a planting scheme — and he did design a number of the community's private gardens and their front yards. One commission in particular allowed Eckbo to realize his ideas on a smaller scale, while extending the limits of materials acceptable in garden construction: the clients would be the family of the landscape architect.

The residence for Arline and Garrett Eckbo was designed by Joseph van der Kar in the modern southern California idiom, in a tone that was neither formulaic nor assertive. Eckbo sought to complement the interior of the house outdoors, with spaces that extended the boundaries of the building toward the hillside. The site occupied land at the intersection of two valleys and required considerable grading to establish suitably level terrain for the house. From the start, Eckbo proposed a series of garden plans, all of which — typical of most designers — he left unrealized, secretly hoping perhaps that the next idea would be even better, and that more money would have accrued for implementation. An early scheme (undated) used a series of geometric shapes, including a lozenge-shaped pool, as fragments set within the graded frame [figure 76]. Sometime in 1956 the Aluminum Company of America, through its advertising agency,

Outdoors-indoors?

Indoors-outdoors?

**75**
The relationship between indoors and out, architecture and landscape architecture.
Carlos Diniz, delineator.
[from Garrett Eckbo, The Art of Home Landscaping]

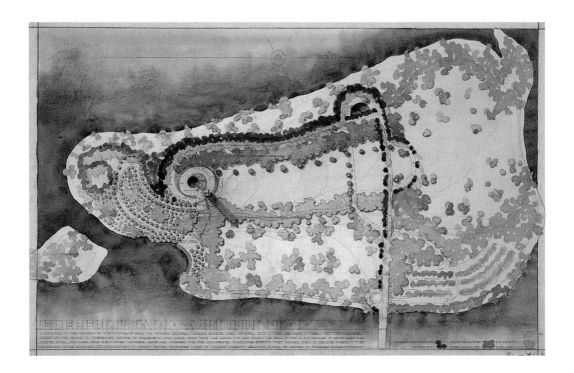

**I**

Freeform Park,
Washington, D.C.
Site plan. Student project
at Harvard University,
1937. Watercolor on
paper.

[*Documents Collection*]

**II**

Arvin Camp, Farm
Security Administration.
circa 1940.
Vernon DeMars, architect.

[*Garrett Eckbo*]

**III**

Mar Vista (Modernique
Homes), Los Angeles, 1948.
Gregory Ain, architect.
The Beethoven Street
landscape today.

[*Marc Treib, 1996*]

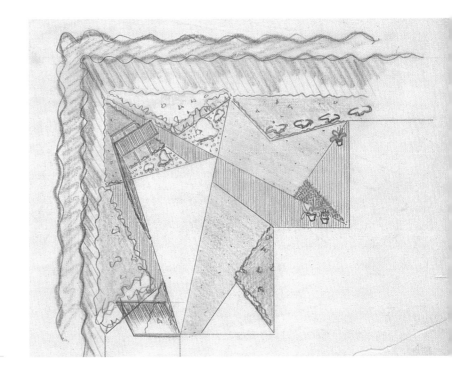

**IV**

Jones garden.
Axonometric study.
Los Angeles, late 1940s.
Colored pencil on tracing
paper.
[*Documents Collection*]

**V**

Sanford garden,
Los Angeles, 1958.
[*Garrett Eckbo*]

**VI**

Goldin garden.
Laurel Canyon, Los
Angeles, mid-1950s.
[*Garrett Eckbo*]

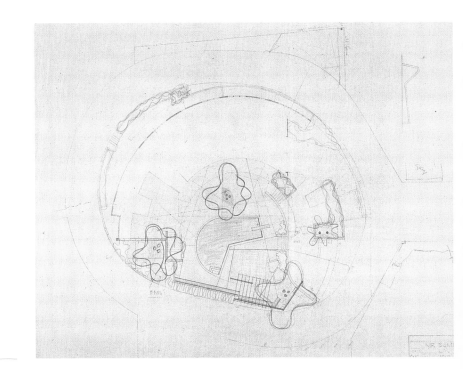

**VII**
Firk garden.
Preliminary plan.
Los Angeles, 1952.
Colored pencil on
diazo print.
[*Documents Collection*]

**VIII**
Sperling garden.
Bel Air, 1949.
Colored pencil on tracing
paper.
[*Documents Collection*]

**IX**
Edmunds garden.
Pacific Palisades, 1956.
[*Garrett Eckbo*]

**X**
Cole garden.
Beverly Hills, early 1950s.
[*Garrett Eckbo*]

**XI**
Cranston swimming pool.
Los Angeles, late 1950s.
[*Garrett Eckbo*]

**XII**

Shulman garden. Court.
Laurel Canyon,
Los Angeles, 1950.
Raphael Soriano,
architect.

[Julius Shulman]

**XIII**
ALCOA Forecast Garden.
View north, toward
house. Laurel Canyon,
Los Angeles, 1959.
[*Julius Shulman*]

**XIV**
ALCOA Forecast Garden.
Aluminum screen walls
and trellis.
Laurel Canyon,
Los Angeles, 1959.
[*Julius Shulman*]

**XV**
Wohlstetter garden.
Pool and screen wall.
Laurel Canyon,
Los Angeles, mid-1950s.
Joseph van der Kar,
architect.

[*Garrett Eckbo*]

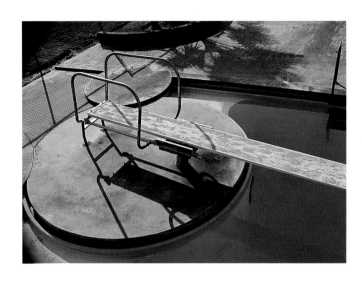

**XVI**
McCormick pool.
Los Angeles, 1950s.

[*Garrett Eckbo*]

**XVII**
Cooper garden.
Bel Air, 1961.

[*Garrett Eckbo*]

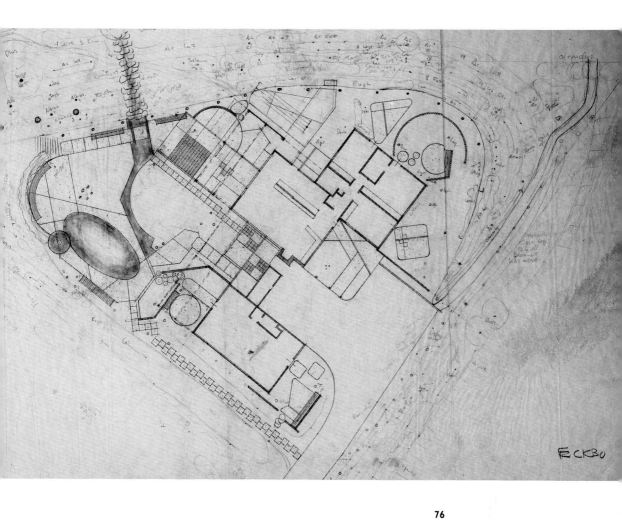

**76**
Eckbo garden.
Laurel Canyon, Los Angeles,
undated, circa 1954.
This unrealized scheme,
which included an elliptical
grassed bed, utilized many
of the landscape architect's
signature elements.
Pencil on tracing paper.
[*Documents Collection*]

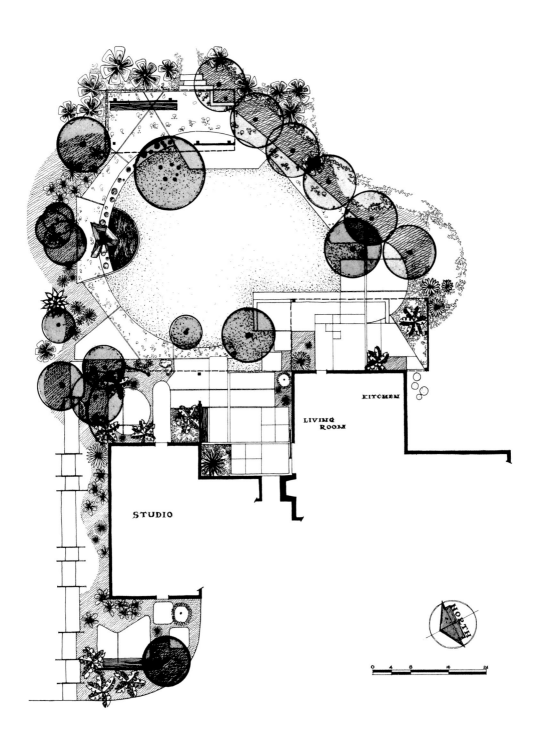

STUDIO

LIVING
ROOM

KITCHEN

NORTH

0    4    8        16        24

contacted Eckbo about the possibility of having him incorporate significant amounts of aluminum in a garden.[99] He agreed to create a metallic garden in his own backyard. The final site plan (construction drawing dated 5 May 1957, but including revisions until 10 March 1959) positioned various screens and their support structures around a broad circle, recalling the suprematist compositions of Kasimir Malevich [figures 77–79]. A smaller circular pad in concrete already existed, used as a patio area outside the studio. A fountain anchored the northeastern edge of the garden design, spilling into a pool whose shape interrupted the purity of the circle. The garden plan in itself was unremarkable, especially when compared to Eckbo's exuberant schemes, from the years on either side of 1950. More remarkable were the materials with which the project was realized [figure 80].

Materials had always been a major consideration in Eckbo's thinking. From the FSA and war housing projects, he had developed a respect for everyday materials. No material was ignoble in itself; the question was how it was used. During the war years, aluminum's widespread application in aviation brought the metal to popular consciousness. Aluminum became the most modern of modern building materials, sold as sheets, beams, and rods to a public anxious to do-it-yourself. Gasoline companies offered aluminum goblets in brilliant or champagne tints with any fill-up. The metal was easy to work, lightweight, and didn't rust. And the reduction in the output of the defense industries challenged manufacturers to invent peacetime applications for their products and production lines. Presumably with hopes of promoting aluminum as an ideal exterior material, ALCOA sponsored the Eckbo garden as a forecast of what might become the domestic landscape of the future.[100]

While no early correspondence remains in the Eckbo office files, the record of a retainer paid in November 1956 testifies to the company's interest in the project. Eckbo's ostensible client was an advertising agency in Pennsylvania — Ketchum, MacLeod and Grove — which acted as the liaison for ALCOA. Although the contractual agreement was finalized years after the project was under way (4 March 1959), its contents clearly revealed the purpose for which the garden was intended: it was a "Display." The research for, and design of, the gar-

**77**
ALCOA Forecast Garden.
Final site plan.
Laurel Canyon,
Los Angeles, 1959.
[*Courtesy Garrett Eckbo*]

**78**
Kasimir Malevich.
*Suprematist Composition,*
*1916–17.*
*[© 1996 Museum of*
*Modern Art, New York]*

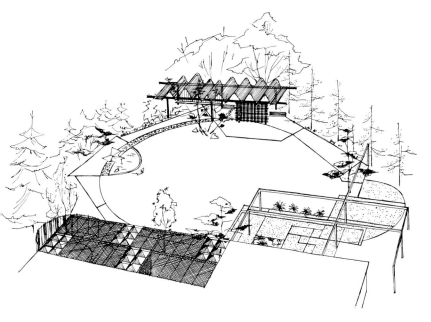

**79**
ALCOA Forecast Garden.
Laurel Canyon,
Los Angeles, 1959.
Aerial sketch view of the
garden.
[*Courtesy Garrett Eckbo*]

**80**
ALCOA Forecast Garden.
Laurel Canyon,
Los Angeles, 1959.
Garrett Eckbo examining
the aluminum pyramids for
the trellis.
[*Julius Shulman*]

den was left within the landscape architect's province. For four months from the announcement of the garden by ALCOA ("April 1960?" is handwritten in the margin), ALCOA was permitted unrestricted use of any of the elements for advertising or merchandising, although the copyright for the design would remain with Garrett Eckbo. From four months to five years, ALCOA retained the right to produce any of the elements of the design, with royalties paid to the designer. Of course, access would be available for ALCOA employees for photography or filming (a promotional film was made). And finally, everything of aluminum had to be made from ALCOA aluminum, a not unreasonable request all things considered.[101]

As described in the ALCOA promotional brochure, aluminum was used in five ways:

1. *A sunbreak that acts as an extension of the living room.*

2. *A one-way screen that affords a view of the planting from the living room, but blocks the view from the studio into the living room and terrace.*

3. *A curved decorative screen designed to demonstrate the possibilities of enclosure.*

4. *A free-standing pavilion shelter, providing a retreat from the main garden area.*

5. *An abstract flower-form fountain that serves as a focal point for the entire group.*

Aluminum, as Eckbo realized, was a nearly ideal product. It was lightweight, soft and easily worked, rustproof and noncorrosive when anodized, particularly in its use as shelter and screening. "One can use a plant or a tree," he said, "or an analogous manufactured device. It is hard to do with wood. It is possible to do it, and do it well, with textiles — but textiles are not durable. For light diffusion, expanded metals are excellent, and no other has the qualities of aluminum."[102] Aluminum colors ranged from garish golds to elegant silvers to muted champagnes. The metal's single disadvantage was its ability to conduct heat, a property not beneficial for the growth of plants on trellis surfaces.

**81**
ALCOA Forecast Garden.
Laurel Canyon,
Los Angeles, 1959.
Trellis and pyramid outside the studio.
[*Julius Shulman*]

Aluminum appeared in the garden principally as a sheet material, most often as expanded mesh. Used both horizontally and vertically it enclosed spaces, provided shade, and overhead formed vaults and pyramids [figures 81, 82; see plate XIV]. Eckbo's curious fountain design, based on a geometrized flower with water spouts as its stamens, was constructed of quarter-inch aluminum plate, crimped, welded, and in places, anodized pale metallic green [see plate XIII]. Aluminum was not used for structural elements, however; wood provided the principal means of support for walls and trellises, as it had traditionally. Wooden frames enclosed the expanded mesh, softening the overall image of the aluminum surfaces, and to some degree naturalizing the manufactured product.

The garden was a publicity triumph and it enjoyed widespread publication in professional, trade, and popular journals and newspapers. While most of the articles drew heavily upon the ALCOA brochure and press release, each biased its reading of the garden according to its audience. "Aluminum invades the garden," shouted *Modern Metals; House and Garden* called it "the shape of shade to come," and saw the design as an escape from a sizzling sun: "You may well be following [Eckbo's] lead yourself in the not too distant summer: first, because the problem of too much sun is one that has plagued a great many home owners besides Mr. Eckbo; second, because the aluminum components that he has adapted to provide shade on his own living patio are standard structural fabrications." If the publication in 1950 of *Landscape for Living* had given Garrett Eckbo national and international prominence within the design professions, the completion of the ALCOA Forecast Garden and its attendant publicity in print and on television brought him widespread popular notoriety.[103]

By 1960 the Eckbo, Royston and Williams partnership no longer existed; the firm was reconstituted as Eckbo, Dean and Williams in 1958.[104] Its arena had become far broader than the individual garden. It planned university campuses, converted streets to pedestrian malls, designed public parks, and studied the policy for open space in all of California. The scope of Eckbo, Dean and Williams' work was constantly increasing, the amount of detailed design necessarily reduced.

The almost manic approach to space and form found in the postwar gardens would never be matched in later designs.

Two decades later, in an interview with Michael Laurie, Eckbo reflected on the importance of garden design in landscape practice:

> There's a snobbery in the profession about gardens as being too small and too inconsequential, but I think that garden design is the real grassroots of landscape design. You encounter all the problems of relations between people and outdoor environment in a concentrated and personal way which brings out all the potentials for very special and forceful kinds of design…. Private garden work is really the only way to find out about relations between people and environment.[105]

In the hundreds of gardens that Garrett Eckbo designed between 1939 and 1959, he had seriously challenged the historical canon of the garden. He did not work in isolation, and his efforts were paralleled by quality and innovative work by landscape architects such as Robert Royston, Lawrence Halprin, Douglas Baylis, Ted Osmundson, and even — if not as continuously — Thomas Church (ten years Eckbo's senior). As a body of work rooted in the residential garden, however, the designs by Eckbo stand alone in number and aesthetic contribution. Certainly, the various configurations of his practice involved far more than residential designs — it encompassed work for community plans, road layouts, parks, shopping centers, schools and colleges, and churches — but the garden has remained at the heart of Eckbo's contribution. By utilizing a contemporary vocabulary drawn from the arts of painting and sculpture, Garrett Eckbo was able to forge spaces and forms that viewers read immediately as modern.

There was a weakness to this approach, however, and Lawrence Halprin has wisely noted the danger in designs that so seriously applied forefront ideas in painting and sculpture to landscape architecture. Halprin cited the Brazilian painter and garden designer Roberto Burle Marx, and his uncanny ability to transfer a pattern to a landscape and have it seem right — although the particular biomorphic shape does not derive from the lay of the land. "In his brilliant hand, the interlocking forms and swirling patterns produced great painterly gardens. In lesser hands," Halprin chided, "his influence, in America and elsewhere for that matter, has resulted in superficially decorative and overly complex parterres with very little organic relation to the landscape or relation to the functioning use of the landscape."[106] The avoidance of applying pattern alone, the transformation of dynamic shapes into dynamic spaces — while maintaining rigorous formal investigation — is another mark of Eckbo's success.

## Epilogue

In 1963 Garrett Eckbo returned to Berkeley as the chair of the Department of Landscape Architecture. This return, he recalls, was bittersweet: sweet in his increased involvement with teaching energetic young student minds, and slightly bitter in having to leave both active practice and southern California. But conditions there had changed: the office was evolving into Eckbo Dean Austin Williams (EDAW), a behemoth of the landscape profession.[107]

But society and the practice of landscape architecture as a whole were also changing. The prosperity and optimism of the immediate postwar era had been transformed into the affluence and social questioning of the 1960s; and then the worldwide civil unrest of 1968. The malevolent products of our ruthless attitude toward the earth were becoming more clear, as agricultural land was churned into suburbia, and water and air quality plummeted. The concern for the planet as a whole, and for the application of a sane ecology, influenced the course of landscape design and enticed it away from the garden. A generation of landscape architects, steeped in the ecological and analytical methods developed by Ian McHarg, retreated from thinking of landscape design as the making of space and form and places in which people live.[108] Nature again was ranked over humanity.

Today, at almost 86, Garrett Eckbo continues to study, think, write, and answer the bothersome questions of nagging would-be biographers. The trail he has blazed through the modern landscape has been both broad and deep, and it leaves a vast field of ideas and designs to be mined by future generations. Indeed, "followers [of Eckbo] have made whole careers out of fragments of his ideas," said landscape architect and professor Laurie Olin, adding: "EDAW has built an empire out of his idea of the corporate practice of interdisciplinary design." But Eckbo remains calm — at least on the surface

—before this adulation, noting that "I wasn't ever aggressive.... Quietly stubborn, maybe. I just did what I wanted to do without arguing."[109] Perhaps this personal evaluation is just a tad too self-effacing. As landscape architect and as author, Garrett Eckbo has been polemical — softly polemical, perhaps, but polemical all the same.

If there is an Eckbo legacy, it tells us that comprehensive considerations, with a stress on the analytical stage of design, do not excuse ugly and unworkable places, whether indoors or out. The garden, the park, the promenade are far more than a few trees for shade and a shelter for eating. Landscape architecture is at root the vehicle by which we improve the relations between people and nature. It is a profession, certainly; it is a discipline, undeniably; and ultimately it is an art, a social art: the social art of landscape design.

## Notes

1   Garrett Eckbo, *Landscape for Living* (New York: Duell, Sloan and Pearce, 1950). Eckbo's thoughts closely paralleled the work of John Brinckerhoff Jackson, the founder of *Landscape* magazine in 1951. Influenced by the French Annales school of geographers, Jackson saw landscape as the product of human activity as well as a visual display: "a composition of man-made or man-modified spaces to serve as infrastructure or background for our collective existence" ("The Word Itself," in *Defining the Vernacular Landscape* [New Haven: Yale University Press, 1984], 8). Jackson rarely spoke of the work of professionally trained landscape architects; instead he focused his acute eye on the vernacular landscape: more pervasive, thus more indicative, of a broader segment of the population. To Jackson, a vernacular landscape was also beautiful and often held more than formal beauty: "The older I grow and the longer I look at landscapes and seek to understand them, the more convinced I am that their beauty is not simply an aspect but their very essence and that that beauty derives from the human presence…. The beauty that we see in the vernacular landscape is the image of our common humanity: hard work, stubborn hope, and mutual forbearance striving to be loved. I believe that a landscape which makes these qualities manifest is one that can be called beautiful" (preface, ibid., xii).

As a designer, Eckbo described at length the tools, intentions, and making of the landscape as well as the everyday and ecological matrix in which the landscape architect worked. These lay at the very root of his argument for a landscape for modern living.

2   In this context a "modernist" manner reflects formal ideas shared with, or adapted from, parallel movements in painting, sculpture, and architecture. One indicator of the dissemination of modern landscape ideas is their widespread publication in popular journals. An example is *Sunset* magazine's *Landscaping for Modern Living* (Menlo Park, Calif.: Lane Publishing, 1956), with its portfolio of work that displays close affinities to the designs of Eckbo, Robert Royston, and Thomas Church, among others.

3   "My father [Axel Eckbo] was one of five brothers and a sister, a family, and he was the nicest and the least competent of all of them. He lost all his money, before they left Norway, in bad investments. After I was born, we went to Chicago where he apparently thought there were some opportunities. In Chicago, he lost all my mother's money in bad investments." (Garrett Eckbo, *Landscape Architecture: The Profession in California, 1935–1940, and Telesis,* interviews conducted by Suzanne B. Riess, 1991 [Berkeley, Calif.: Regional Oral History Project, 1993], 1–2). Eckbo's mother, Theodora Munn, was from Cooperstown, in upstate New York, and had met her husband while traveling in Norway. They lived there for seven years: "She became pregnant, and for some reason decided to come back to the States so I would be born here, which was probably fortunate" (ibid., 1).

4   "He had a big house on a hill and a Rolls Royce and a chauffeur and three horses and stuff like that…. He was the kind of a man who would always get rich no matter where he was or what happened to him" (ibid., 2–3). Eckbo would stay in Norway about six months, learn of the stock market crash while there, and return to California with a new sense of dedication. A denial by his uncle to provide funding for school, unless his academic standing improved, led Eckbo to junior college. In later years, at Berkeley and Harvard, Uncle Eivind would provide some financial support for his studies (conversation with the authors, Berkeley, 31 May 1996).

5   *An Interview with Garrett Eckbo,* January 1981, conducted by Michael Laurie, ed. Karen Madsen (Watertown, Mass.: Hubbard Educational Trust, 1990), 2.

6   Little of the Olmsted scheme had been implemented, and even less of it remains today, principally the curving and divided Piedmont Avenue on the eastern side of the campus.

An international competition in 1897 had solicited a more monumental campus plan, won by the French Beaux-Arts architect Émile Bénard. The design's formal axis descended the hillside, crossed by a secondary axis, and flanked by green spaces seemingly more in the English than the French tradition. Bénard declined the invitation to realize his scheme (his wife, it is said, had no interest in encountering bears firsthand); John Galen Howard (1864–1931), the fourth-place prize winner (with engineer Samuel Cauldwell), became campus planner and later dean of the school of architecture.

7   Born in 1880, Gregg was a New Englander who had worked in the office of the Olmsted Brothers on their project for the 1904 Louisiana Purchase Exposition held in St. Louis — like the 1893 Columbian Exposition in Chicago, planned with the precepts of Beaux-Arts classicism. For a comprehensive history of the landscape architecture department see Michael Laurie, with David Streatfield, *75 Years of Landscape Architecture at Berkeley: An Informal History. Part I: The First 50 Years* (Berkeley: Department of Landscape Architecture, University of California, 1988), 4–5.

"Miss Jones was not only the logical person to teach plant materials, but was the only one at the time trained in the work." Katherine Jones was born in Wisconsin in 1860, and came to California when she was twenty, majored in botany and biology, and graduated in 1896. She taught in the department for several decades (ibid., 5–6).

*Curriculum of University of California College Bulletin*, ca. 1914, cited in Laurie, *75 Years*, 10.

8   Laurie, *75 Years*, 27–28.

9   Helen Hunt Jackson, *Ramona* (New York: Grosset and Dunlap, 1884). Harold Kirker explains: "For the Californians were uncertainly discovering that they had a past of their own. As one of them put it: 'Give me neither Romanesque nor Gothic; much less Italian Renaissance, and least of all English Colonial — this is California — Give me Mission' " (as quoted in Felix Rey, "A Tribute to Mission Style," *Architect and Engineer* [October 1924]: 78). More succinctly: "An immigrant society is always culturally conservative" (*California's Architectural Frontier: Style and Tradition in the Nineteenth Century* [Santa Barbara: Peregrine Smith, 1973], 130).

10   See Marc Treib, "Aspects of Regionality and the Modern(ist) Garden in California," in *Regional Garden Design in the United States*, ed. Therese O'Malley and Marc Treib (Washington, D.C.: Dumbarton Oaks, 1995), 5-42.

11   Marion Hollins — client, developer and celebrated golfer — may have truncated the designers' ambitions. Daniel Gregory notes: "No tree could be removed to make way for the golf course without her personal permission. She established small parks along the creek beds and in the heavily forested sections… [and] drew up a list of protective restrictions which, according to the advertising brochure of 1930, 'will go with the land, assuring maintenance to the purchaser of the character of the surroundings as to trees, shrubs and individuality' " ("Pasatiempo," in John Chase, *A Sidewalk Companion to Santa Cruz Architecture* [Santa Cruz: Paper Visions Press, 1979], 295–96).

Wurster shared Church's interest in the Mediterranean region as a source for California architecture and landscape design, although both were touched by the modernist current that moved west. For a discussion of the parallels between their two careers, see Dorothée Imbert, "Of Gardens and Houses as Places to Live: Thomas Church and William Wurster," and Marc Treib, "A Feeling for Function,"

both in *An Everyday Modernism: The Houses of William Wurster*, ed. Marc Treib (Berkeley: University of California Press, 1995), 114–37 and 12–83, respectively.

12   *An Interview with Garrett Eckbo*, 2.

13   January, 1935, Berkeley student project. Eckbo papers, College of Environmental Design Documents Collection, University of California at Berkeley (hereafter, Eckbo papers, Documents Collection). Eckbo explains that the name of the country club was fabricated, "got rocks" being the contemporary slang term for the wealthy. This may be the only golf course he ever designed (conversation with the authors, Berkeley, 25 February 1996).

14   *An Interview with Garrett Eckbo*, 3. The perspective drawing is dated 18 April 1934 (Project Archives, Department of Landscape Architecture, University of California at Berkeley). The design draws more inspiration from the landscape architect than from the king who was his patron. The project should more accurately be termed "in the manner of André le Nôtre." Unlike Eckbo, his classmate Dan Kiley to this very day regards le Nôtre as his "hero."

Three splayed paths, roads, or allées converge on (or conversely, radiate from) a single point; known in French as the *patte-d'oie* (goose foot). The planning device was used in garden as well as urban planning: the best known examples are Versailles, outside Paris, and the Piazza del Popolo, in Rome.

15   The plan is dated 19 June 1935 (Eckbo papers, Documents Collection).

16   "As far as can be ascertained, practically every landscape architect (within the membership of the ASLA) who is not otherwise employed in private practice and who has had sufficient experience to warrant his acceptance of definite designing responsibilities, is now employed in Government work. This proportion of the heretofore unemployed membership approx-

imates 90 per cent" (A.D.T., "Notes on Federal Activities Relating to Landscape Architecture," *Landscape Architecture* [October 1934]: 41).

17   Eckbo worked under the senior landscape architect J. A. Gooch. "His other duties included advising customers on planting and maintenance for a range of microclimates from mountains to beaches and deserts" (Melanie Simo, "The Education of a Modern landscape Designer," *Pacific Horticulture* [Summer 1988]: 26). Conversation with the author, 7 January 1996, and letter to the authors, 28 May 1996. How many of the sites Eckbo actually saw before designing, and how many were realized, remain open to question.

18   Conversation with the authors, 25 February 1996. In 1939 *Sunset* magazine sponsored a house and garden designed for a representative group of 300 members of the Berkeley Women's City Club. The architect, Clarence Mayhew, produced a house design that became even more bland after a review meeting held en masse with the putative clients ("Sunset and 300 Western Women Build a Home," *Sunset*, March 1939, 20–21; "300 Western Women Start Planning Sunset House," *Sunset* [April 1939]: 48–49, and May 1939, 34–35).

The garden, by H. L. and Adele Vaughan, was planned as a "distinctive" and "always presentable" design that offered sun with a spot of shade, space for the dog, a pleasant view from the kitchen, and brick terraces off the living and breakfast rooms — all to be maintained with minimal care. In character, the garden was not unlike those planned by Eckbo during his year in Los Angeles: each function of the design has its space, and a sense of informality prevails ("Come Into the Garden: 300 Western Women Present the Garden Plan for Sunset House," *Sunset*, June 1939, 36–37).

The house was further revised due to economics ("Sunset House: Revised to Meet the Budget," *Sunset*, October 1939, 27).

19   Eckbo recalls that the clients usually wanted one of each fruit — "Southern California exuberance," as he called it (letter to the authors, 28 May 1996).

20   Conversation with the authors, Berkeley, 25 February 1996.

21   *An Interview with Garrett Eckbo*, 3.

22   "Arline came east to spend the summer with her parents in White Plains [New York], having graduated from San Francisco State College. …Just before the new year began at Harvard, we were married — in a minister's living room in New York City — and went happily off to Cambridge" (letter to the authors, 28 May 1996).

Arline Williams was born in Pittsburgh, Pennsylvania, where her father worked for the General Cable company. She was the oldest of four children, followed by Edward and Albert, and then Carol. A reassignment by the firm caused the family's removal to the Bay Area in 1929, where Arline studied English first at the University of California at Berkeley and then at San Francisco State University. She graduated in winter 1937, after Eckbo had begun his graduate study at Harvard.

The Eckbo's daughter Marilyn (Kweskin) was born in 1941, Alison (Peper) three years later. There are now six grandchildren (conversations with the authors, Berkeley, 10 May 1996, and 31 May 1996).

23   Eugene Bressler, "Chronological summary, history of the Department of Landscape Architecture" (Cambridge, Mass.: Department of Landscape Architecture, Harvard University, 1970), 8. I am grateful to Mary F. Daniels, Special Collections Librarian of the Loeb Library at Harvard, for providing me with a copy of this publication.

24   Henry Vincent Hubbard and Theodora Kimball, *Introduction to the Study of Landscape Design* (New York: Macmillan, 1917), 30–31. The book had four reprintings in the next two decades and revised editions in 1929 and 1938.

25   Eckbo, *Landscape for Living*, 12–19; Garrett Eckbo, "Outdoors and In: Gardens as Living Space," *Magazine of Art* 34, no. 5 (October 1941): 425.

26   Reuben Rainey, " 'Organic Form in the Humanized Landscape': Garrett Eckbo's Landscape for Living," in *Modern Landscape Architecture*, ed. Treib, 180–205.

27   Reacting to the conclusion of the book's preface, Eckbo wrote: "Theory and practice [are] both essential — inspired designers are bunk" (viii); he later added, responding to the discussion of taste: "Who cares? Nuts to ye great artist — individual ego rampant" (29). He also took umbrage at the soothing naturalistic balm of the Olmsted park: "Olmsted takes for granted that towns must be hard & hustling" (18), an opinion he did not share. Against the subhead "Choice of Style": "He completely takes for granted that we must make this, that we can use these now; 20th century U.S.A.; My God!" (60). Eckbo's comments taper off after the first third of the book, perhaps owing to fatigue, perhaps to the authors' reduced number of aesthetic and philosophical pronouncements and greater examination of the materials with which landscapes are made. I am grateful to Garrett Eckbo for allowing me access to his copy of Hubbard and Kimball's text.

28   In 1935, "The President and Overseers of Harvard University establish the Graduate School of Design, uniting Schools of Architecture, Landscape Architecture, and City Planning under one Faculty and Dean. Reasons for the reorganization include combining the financial

resources and 'providing an enhanced association among students in the allied fields'" (Bressler, "Chronological summary," 8). Joseph Hudnut, preface to Walter Gropius, *The New Architecture and the Bauhaus*, trans. P. Morton Shand (London: Faber and Faber, n.d.), 7.

29   Eckbo, *Landscape for Living*, 6. He introduced chapter 9, "Spacing for Living — People on the Land," thus: "People live ON the earth, ON the land, but IN the three-dimensional air-space, the atmospheric volume, immediately above this land surface" (ibid., 61).

30   Walter Gropius, "Is There a Science of Design?" (1947), in *Scope of Total Architecture* (New York: Harper and Row, 1955), 20; and also the chapter "Scope of Total Architecture," 171.

31   Christopher Tunnard, *Gardens in the Modern Landscape* (1938; revised ed., London: Architectural Press, 1948), 88. When this revised edition was published, Tunnard had relocated to the United States and turned almost exclusively to broader issues of city planning, but the book retained its currency and was highly regarded well into the 1960s. For a comparison of the content of the two editions, see Lance Neckar, "Strident Modernism / Ambivalent Reconsiderations: Christopher Tunnard's *Gardens in the Modern Landscape*," *Journal of Garden History* 10 (1990): 237–46. And for an overview of Tunnard's ideas and career, see Lance Neckar, "Christopher Tunnard: The Garden in the Modern Landscape," in *Modern Landscape Architecture*, ed. Treib, 145–58.

32   Christopher Tunnard, "Modern Gardens for Modern Houses: Reflections on Current Trends in Landscape Design," in *Modern Landscape Architecture*, ed. Treib, 162.

33   Project for a Country Estate, 1937 (Eckbo papers, Documents Collection). In 1939, after Eckbo's

graduation, the landscape architecture curriculum was revised, because "the profession's most significant future lies in the area of public work and of large scale physical planning" (Bressler, Chronological summary," 9).

34   The watercolor board for the project is dated 1 November 1937; the planting plan, 16 November (Eckbo papers, Documents Collection).

35   Freeform Park, site plan (ibid.).

36   Gropius had written that "whereas building is merely a matter of methods and materials, architecture implies the mastery of space" (*The New Architecture and the Bauhaus*, 20). Space, with a concomitant reduction in mass, was a preoccupation of modernist architects. This message recurred in Eckbo's published writings almost from the beginning, for example: "Space, in the present context, means the layer of air above the surface of the earth in which people live, work, and play" (Garrett Eckbo, "Landscape Design in the USA," *Architectural Review* [January 1949]: 25). Even late in life, Eckbo holds that space links architecture and landscape with engineering in a single quest: "The Professions too will need to reorganize. The planning arts, the spatial design arts (architecture, engineering, landscape architecture, interior design), the object / furniture / utilities arts, the communication / performing arts will all need consolidation, reorganization, and reinvigoration" ("Pilgrim's Progress," in *Modern Landscape Architecture*, ed. Treib, 219). See also note 29.

37   James C. Rose, "Freedom in the Garden: A Contemporary Approach in Landscape Design," *Pencil Points* (October 1938): 639.

38   Henry-Russell Hitchcock and Philip Johnson, *The International Style* (1932; reprint, New York: W. W. Norton, 1966). In Lao Tzu's words,

"Adapt the nothing therein to the purpose in hand, and you will have the use of the cart. Knead clay in order to make a vessel. Adapt the nothing therein to the purpose in hand, and you will have the use of the vessel. Cut out doors and windows in order to make a room. Adapt the nothing therein to the purpose in hand, and you will have the use of the room" (Lao Tzu, *Tao Te Ching*, trans. D. C. Lau [Baltimore: Penguin Books, 1963], 67).

39   Garrett Eckbo, "Sculpture & Landscape Design," *Magazine of Art* 31, no. 4 (April 1938): 202.

40   Alfred Barr, *Cubism and Abstract Art* (New York: Museum of Modern Art, 1936), 13.

41   Although this lacuna was endemic across modernist design — attested by its omission from the Bauhaus curriculum — Barr sought an appropriate setting for the paintings and sculpture in his collection. New York's Museum of Modern Art opened its new building by Philip L. Goodwin and Edward D. Stone in May 1939, and its first sculpture garden. Barr attempted to introduce some aspect of modern art into the garden's design. Working quickly in collaboration with Barr, John McAndrew, then curator of Architecture and Design, devised a scheme with thin walls — both straight and waving planes to define space — within and against which the sculpture was displayed. The existing (although altered) garden court was constructed in 1953 to designs by Philip Johnson and followed a more pristine and sophisticated tone. See Mirka Beneš, "Inventing a Modern Sculpture Garden in 1939 at the Museum of Modern Art, New York," *Landscape Journal* (Spring 1994): 1–20.

42   Fletcher Steele, "New Pioneering in Garden Design," *Landscape Architecture* (April 1930): 158–77. Dorothée Imbert discusses the impact of the modernist French garden designers in "A Model for

Modernism: The Work and Influence of Pierre-Émile Legrain," in *Modern Landscape Architecture*, ed. Treib, 92–107. A comparison of Eckbo's sketch and its photographic source appears as figures 11-10 and 11-11. For a complete discussion of French garden design in the first half of the twentieth century, see Dorothée Imbert, *The Modernist Garden in France* (New Haven: Yale University Press, 1993). *The Works of Garrett Eckbo: Landscape for Living*, ed. Warren T. Byrd, Jr., Proceedings of the Second Annual Symposium on Landscape Architecture, 11 February 1984 (Charlottesville: Division of Landscape Architecture, University of Virginia, 1987), 8.

Eckbo was probably unaware of the *yatsuhashi* (zigzag bridge) found in Japanese gardens. The overlay of planks at angled intersections may reflect the belief that evil spirits move only in straight lines; its bent path coerces visitors to continually modify their view.

43   Eckbo, "Sculpture & Landscape Design," 206. Both Rose and Eckbo would mine *Cubism and Abstract Art* to illustrate their own writing. Dan Kiley used a similar movement in his project for the "cherry sweep" at Waverly Oaks, where the visitor descends the earthen spiral to approach a pool set at its center. See Margaret Olthof Goldsmith, *Designs for Outdoor Living* (New York: George W. Stewart, 1941), 282–87.

44   While his designs were less influential after the mid-1960s, James C. Rose's early writings exerted a large impact on young professionals, students, and architects. Dan Kiley's long and distinguished career continues to this day, engaged more in practice than writing. See Gregg Bleam, "Modern and Classical Themes in the Work of Dan Kiley," in *Modern Landscape Architecture*, ed. Treib, 220–39; *Landscape Design: Works of Dan Kiley; Process Architecture #33* (October 1982); *Dan Kiley:*

*Landscape Design II: In Step with Nature, Process Architecture #108* (February 1993); Calvin Tomkins, "The Garden Artist," *New Yorker*, 16 October 1995, 136–47.

45   Garrett Eckbo, Daniel U. Kiley, James C. Rose, "Landscape Design in the Primeval Environment," *Architectural Record* (May 1939): 79. The accompanying articles ran in the August 1939 and February 1940 issues.

46   James C. Rose, "Gardens," *California Arts and Architecture* (May 1940): 20.

47   Gropius, *The New Architecture and the Bauhaus*, 18.

48   Tunnard, *Gardens in the Modern Landscape*, 62.

49   James C. Rose, "Why Not Try Science?," *Pencil Points* (December 1939): 777–79. In his designs for "Modular Gardens" (*Progressive Architecture* [September 1947]: 76–80), Rose presented a series of structures that could be used in a variety of settings, as well as a plant list charted by height and season.

50   Eckbo, *Landscape for Living*, 1–3. For the quotation from Christopher Cauldwell (*Illusion and Reality* [New York: International Publishers, 1947]), Eckbo gives no specific page.

51   For a further discussion of the role of the arts in the development of modernist landscape architecture see Imbert, "A Model for Modernism," 92–107, and Marc Treib, "Axioms for a Modern Landscape Architecture," in *Modern Landscape Architecture*, ed. Treib, 36–67.

52   Joan Miró, *Je travaille comme un jardinier* (Paris: Société Internationale d'Art du XXᵉ Siècle, 1964), 42. See also James Thrall Soby, *Joan Miró* (New York: Museum of Modern Art, 1959).

53   Garrett Eckbo, "Small Gardens in the City," *Pencil Points* (September 1937). A note at the bottom of a

drawing established the design period: "Made by Garrett Eckbo at Harvard University at ten scale from April 11 to May 12, 1937 — so help me, so help me, so help me" (Eckbo papers, Documents Collection).

54   Eckbo, "Pilgrim's Progress," 208–9.

55   This deformation of a commonly held lot line became an Eckbo tool in later residential community work, softening the edge between adjacent properties.

56   Eckbo, "Pilgrim's Progress," 209.

57   Eckbo, *Landscape for Living*, 175.

58   Ibid. The preliminary site plan is dated 22 March 1938, ink drawings followed in June (Eckbo papers, Documents Collection). Text from "Detail Plans, Lots 4-12-20," dated 7 June 1938. Original drawing missing, film negative in the Eckbo papers, Documents Collection.

59   Conversation with the authors, Berkeley, 25 February 1996.

60   The text paraphrases Eckbo's own description and gives the design prominence and legibility (Goldsmith, *Designs for Outdoor Living*, 114–18).

61   "Landscape Gardening II: Community Planting," *Architectural Forum* (March 1946): 141.

62   Eckbo papers, Documents Collection.

63   "In retrospect, it is obvious that I over-designed that job. All of the action was intended to be on the inside of the building. On the outside it was a blank shell, however freeform. Geddes [primarily an industrial designer] had an architect running the job. Eventually, they brought in an elderly landscape architect colleague, who planted some mature elms around the building. It was an interesting exer-

cise in the study of pure form. We are grateful to General Motors for that opportunity" (Garrett Eckbo, letter to the authors, 28 May 1996).

64   John Steinbeck, *The Grapes of Wrath* (1939; reprint, New York: Penguin Books, 1967), 44.

65   Eckbo describes the office as having "30 engineers, 20 architects and 3 landscape architects. Burton Cairns and Vernon DeMars were District Architects, Herbert Hallsteen, District Engineer (our boss). John Steinbeck's *The Grapes of Wrath* was our Bible" (letter to the authors, 28 May 1996).

66   Michael C. Steiner, "Regionalism in the Great Depression," *The Geographical Review* 73, no. 4 (October 1983): 433. And Steinbeck, *The Grapes of Wrath*, 113–15.

67   Arno Cammerer, in Albert H. Good, *Park and Recreation Structures* (Washington, D. C.: Department of the Interior, National Park Service, 1938), vii.

68   Steiner, "Regionalism in the Great Depression," 435. Eckbo wrote, "There was never really a 'regional or traditional expression' specified. Budget and functional limits were strict. The few buildings were strictly functional" (letter to the authors, 28 May 1996).

69   For a critical biography of Lange, which includes discussion for her work with the Farm Security Administration, see Therese Thau Heyman, Sandra S. Phillips, John Szarkowski, *Dorothea Lange: American Photographs* (San Francisco: San Francisco Museum of Modern Art; Chronicle Books, 1994).

70   *Task*, no. 6 (winter 1944–45). Eckbo was also the West Coast correspondent for the magazine, which was based in Cambridge, Massachusetts.

71   Peter Reed, "Enlisting Modernism," in *World War II and the American Dream*, ed. Donald Albrecht (Washington, D.C.: National Building Museum; Cambridge, Mass.: MIT Press, 1995), 11

72   Eckbo describes Burton Cairns: "I think he was one of the wiser people [in Telesis]. He didn't have quite the flair that Vernon [DeMars] has, the sort of, you can call it design flair, design identity. Which is not necessarily very important, except to designers to argue about. But he was very solid socially. A very good citizen" (Eckbo, *Landscape Architecture*, 47).

73   "1949: The total number of homes built since January 1946 reaches five-point-one million" (Heather Burnham and Joel Davidson, "Chronology," in *World War II and the American Dream*, ed. Albrecht, xli).

74   Edward Williams was born in Pittsburgh in 1914, but the family moved to the San Francisco Bay area in 1929. He was Eckbo's classmate at the University of California at Berkeley, graduating in 1935. After graduation he worked for the noted, if older-generation, landscape architects Butler Sturtevant and E. L. Kiler in Palo Alto. His interests always seemed to have been broadscale, and he served as a consultant to the San Mateo County Recreation and Planning Commissions. "A skillful designer, Williams had placed second in the national competition that sent Eckbo to Harvard. But as the firm grew, Williams assumed more responsibilities in management and planning. For his partners and younger associates, he remained a stabilizing influence – a rock of integrity in a fluid, changing world" (Peter Walker and Melanie Simo, *Invisible Gardens* [Cambridge, Mass.: MIT Press, 1994], 133). He died in 1984.

75   Royston took an active role in the planning of the Ladera community on the San Francisco peninsula

(Robert Royston, "Point of View / Robert Royston," *Landscape Architecture* [November–December 1986]: 66); and Robert Royston, "A Brief History," *Landscape Australia* (Summer 1986): 34–36.

76   "A Professional Adventure in Use of Outdoor Space," *Architect and Engineer* (September 1946), 11.

77   See Esther McCoy, *Modern California Houses: Case Study Houses 1945–1962* (New York: Reinhold, 1962); and Elizabeth A. T. Smith, curator, Howard Singerman, ed., *Blueprints for Modern Living: History and Legacy of the Case Study Houses* (Los Angeles: Museum of Contemporary Art; Cambridge, Mass.: MIT Press, 1989).

78   Simo, "The Education of a Modern Landscape Designer," 26. For a sense of the previous decade, see also David Gebhard and Harriette von Breton, *L.A. in the Thirties, 1931–1941* (Salt Lake City: Peregrine Smith, 1975). Also Esther McCoy, *The Second Generation* (Salt Lake City: Gibbs Smith, 1984).

79   Eckbo, *Landscape Architecture*, 75. See also letter to the authors, 12 January 1996. They moved several times between the years 1946 and 1952, when they settled in their home in Wonderland Park (conversation with the authors, Berkeley, 31 May 1996).

80   Michael Laurie, "The Modern California Garden," *Pacific Horticulture* (Summer 1993): 23. Although Eckbo's vocabulary was drastically different from his British colleague's, the play between architectural structure and planting was not unlike that of the Edwin Lutyens-Gertrude Jekyll collaborations. Lutyens, as architect, usually established the walls, primary spaces, and the designs of features such as pergolas. Jekyll designed the often complex plantings — herbaceous borders, for example — that effaced the precise edges of the architecture, added seasonal variety,

a sense of life, and an intermediary material between stone and the human body. Characteristic projects include the Deanery Garden (1899), Lindisfarne Castle (1903–1907), and Hestercombe (1904–1909). For discussion of the Jekyll-Lutyens "partnership," see Jane Brown, *Gardens of a Golden Afternoon* (London: Penguin Books, 1982).

81  Wassily Kandinsky, *On the Spiritual in Art*, trans. M.T.H. Sadler (1914; reprint, New York: Dover Publications, 1977), 32, 49.

82  Ibid., 30–31.

83  Paul Klee, *Pedagogical Sketchbook*, trans. Sibyl Moholy-Nagy (1925; New York: Frederick Praeger, 1977), 59.

84  The project was not realized. Wistfully (and with tongue in cheek) Eckbo bemoans: "My one crack at a large estate design and it didn't get built" (conversation with the authors, Berkeley, 18 May 1996).

85  Klee, *Pedagogical Sketchbook*, 53.

86  Garrett Eckbo, *The Art of Home Landscaping* (New York: McGraw-Hill, 1956), 261, 265, 266.

87  Goldsmith, *Designs for Outdoor Living*, 201. John Cheever, "The Swimmer," in *The Stories of John Cheever* (New York: Ballantine Books, 1982), 714.

88  Thomas Church quotes the sixteenth-century English philosopher Francis Bacon, "Of Gardens": "Pooles marre all, and make the garden unwholsome and full of Flies, and Frogs" (*Gardens Are for People* [New York: Reinhold, 1955], 217).

89  For a discussion of the Thomas Church-Lawrence Halprin design for the Donnell garden, see Treib, "Aspects of Regionality and the Modern(ist) Garden in California."

90  Eckbo, "Landscape Design in the USA," 25.

91  Eckbo, *The Art of Home Landscaping*, 197; Eckbo, *Landscape for Living*, 152.

92  See Treib, "Axioms for a Modern Landscape Architecture," 47–53.

93  Connections among the members of the northern California artistic community were quite strong from the late 1930s on. These social bonds were furthered by the efforts of the San Francisco Museum of Art to include active programs in architecture, landscape architecture, and design with those of painting, prints, and sculpture. In 1937 the first international survey of contemporary landscape architecture was held at the museum, followed by similar exhibitions in 1948 and 1958. During the 1940s and 1950s the Eckbo, Royston and Williams offices worked with several artists, the principal one being Claire Falkenstein. Thomas Church's collaboration with Adaline Kent for the pool sculpture for the Donnell garden is well documented; in 1938 Church had also worked with Florence Allston Swift on a garden project for the "Exhibition of Mural Conceptualism" at the museum. See David Streatfield, *California Gardens: Creating a New Eden* (New York: Abbeville Press, 1994), 190–201.

94  Eckbo, "Landscape Design in the USA," 25. This thinking continues the idea of the "structural" use of plants described above, and it was given renewed attention in *Landscape for Living*, published the following year. Garrett Eckbo, "The Esthetics of Planting," in *Landscape Design* (San Francisco: San Francisco Museum of Art, 1948), 17.

95  Eckbo, "The Esthetics of Planting," 17–18.

96  Eckbo, *Landscape for Living*, 149. See also Eckbo, *The Art of Home Landscaping*, 42, 127–41.

97  This rooting in practice did not escape the notice of one reviewer: "Even though this book is almost exclusively concerned with theory, it is the theory of a doer, of the essentially creative person" (Robert W. Kennedy, review of *Landscape for Living*, *Architectural Record* [August 1950]: 28).

98  About twelve families at first, up to sixty families over time (conversation with the authors, Berkeley, 31 May 1996). The date of the garden is difficult to fix precisely. Documents suggest that the project had been in Eckbo's mind since the middle of the decade, but that its realization took about five years. The contractual agreement between the landscape architect and ALCOA, dated 4 March 1959, referred to a letter of 16 October 1956 from Eckbo to ALCOA's agents Ketchum, MacLeod and Grove; Eckbo office records show a retainer received on 2 November 1956, when the design of the project probably began in earnest.

Three sheets of the construction drawings for the garden — which appear to be a set of six sheets — bear the date of 30 May 1957; the fountain drawing, 25 November 1958. A document from the Los Angeles Department of Building and Safety dated 20 January 1959 — marked "This is not a building permit," and listing additional drawings required for permission to build — suggests that the design was nearly ready for construction; the fountain drawings may not have accompanied the first, or any other, submission.

The realized garden first appeared in the April 1960 issues of several publications. From slides (dated November 1959) taken by Eckbo during a promotional photo shoot, we estimate late 1959 as the date of the garden's "completion" (ALCOA Garden File, Eckbo papers, Documents Collection).

99  When asked why ALCOA had selected him as designer, Eckbo replied — ironically, and with a chuckle: "I guess because I was so 'famous' " (conversation with the authors, Berkeley, 9 May 1996).

100  Aluminum was the most publicized material in the ALCOA Forecast Garden but not necessarily the most unusual. In the construction drawings, Eckbo called for "a new pebbly concrete" that contained equal parts of Lomita gravel; crushed red sewer tile, and beach pebbles. He also used sections of tile sewer pipe, set vertically in concrete slabs, as planters for succulents (construction drawings, Plot Plan, 30 May 1957, ALCOA Garden File, Eckbo papers, Documents Collection).

ALCOA also sponsored an aluminum house at the 1960 Triennale in Milan, Italy, although the company was hardly alone in marketing its products through futuristic projects. Monsanto Chemical Company, for example, sponsored a plastic house in 1955, later relocated to Disneyland in Anaheim, California, and rechristened the Disneyland Monsanto House of the Future.

101  A film introducing the garden was shown on ABC television on 21 June [1960?]. Printed announcement and 4 March 1959 letter of agreement between Aluminum Company of America and Garrett Eckbo are in ALCOA Garden File, Eckbo papers, Documents Collection.

102  *FORECAST LA.NDSCAPE*, n.d., n.p. (Eckbo papers, Documents Collection).

103  "The Shape of Shade to Come," *House and Garden*, April 1960, 155. In a retrospective explanatory note accompanying a photograph, Eckbo reflected on the garden's design: "I liked it. But there has been no aluminum renaissance in American gardens — outside of California, only profound conservatism" (Eckbo to Marc Treib, ca. Autumn 1992).

Today (May 1996) little remains of the aluminum elements of the garden except one wall of the north arbor, now painted a dull brown. Over the years, at the hands of successive owners, a curiously shaped swimming pool and floral planting have appeared; the fountain has been removed; the trees planted in the mid-1950s grew to overwhelm the space. The space, however, keeps some of its original character, and the principal paved surfaces — now uplifted by tree roots — are still in place.

Eckbo has consulted with at least two later owners, after visits to the site at their request. His comments were directed only toward pruning, maintenance, and planting — he did not mention the ideas that took root on that site 40 years ago (letters from Garrett Eckbo to Owner #1, 26 November 1987, and Owners #2, 25 June 1989).

104  The partnership was dissolved in 1958 and divided into the southern branch, Eckbo, Dean and Williams, and the northern branch, Royston, Hanamato and Mayes.

105  *An Interview with Garrett Eckbo*, 12.

106  Lawrence Halprin, "The Last 40 Years: A personal Overview of Landscape Architecture in America," *Space Design*, Special Issue 1984; *Gardens: Wonderland of Contrivance and Illusion*, 5 (English translation). The Brazilian artist's landscapes should be distinguished from the painterly gardens of the English landscape grand tradition. There, garden makers employed the framing and compositional devices of artists who composed views of landscapes. The weakness of many modern (and postmodern) garden designers is that they reapplied a two-dimensional design (a plan) to the garden with little three-dimensional, that is, spatial development. See Treib, "Axioms for a Modern Landscape Architecture." For an

extended discussion of the garden as visual object (*tableau-jardin*) and its limitations, see Imbert, *The Modernist Garden in France*.

107  The firm was incorporated in 1968; Eckbo left EDAW in 1973 ("after an 18 months' controversy over organizational policies and procedures"), and "returned to a small private practice scale" (*An Interview with Garrett Eckbo*, 20, 15).

108  See Ian McHarg, *Design with Nature* (Garden City, N.Y.: Doubleday, 1966).

109  Cited by J. William Thompson, "Standard-Bearer of Modernism," *Landscape Architecture* (February 1990): 89, 90.

Firebaugh Unit.
Row Housing.
San Joaquin Valley,
1939–1940.
Farm Security
Administration.

[*Documents Collection*]

# THE ART OF SOCIAL LANDSCAPE DESIGN

## Dorothée Imbert

For almost six decades Garrett Eckbo gave form to our landscape. The scope of his contributions ranged from small sculptural gardens to large-scale planning schemes; his practice evolved from a home-based studio enterprise to a multi-initialed corporation. Eckbo's commitment to aesthetics, laid upon solid social foundations, never wavered. To the self-posed rhetorical questions — Is design social? and Is it art? — he replied, "Formal design can be socially oriented and social design may be art. Regardless of form concepts, the basic question may be: is design for people, or are people a vehicle for design?"[1]

From the outset of his career, Eckbo treated plants both as units of construction and as conductors for social patterns, whether they structured the private realm or the collective landscape. No matter how elite, his gardens were always considered to be arenas for living, rather than mere pictorial compositions. Perhaps even more remarkable was his double dedication to create a new form of community life and instill beauty in the landscapes for the landless laborers of the depression. William Wurster, architect and longtime collaborator of Thomas Church, commended architects who "*chose* to work for the Government," in particular Burton Cairns and Vernon DeMars, for their design of the Farm Security Administration migrant camps in California. Wurster assessed camps as "minimum shelters for human beings [that had become] 'architecture.'" With such endeavors, he

Garrett Eckbo.
Southern California,
circa 1946.
[Documents Collection]

continued, "the design of buildings emerged as a social art, and [he] hope[d] it will never be placed exclusively on the luxury shelf again."[2] Similarly, Eckbo's contribution to the New Deal landscape remains an extraordinary conjunction of high design, or art, and true understanding of social exchanges — and people.

The projects Eckbo conceived for the Farm Security Administration mark the first concrete manifestation of his involvement in designing the collective landscape. Student projects and early publications had already demonstrated the telltale signs of a growing social conscience. His writings from 1938 onward are informed with an awareness of the disproportionate distribution of wealth, the tension between aesthetics and functionalism, and the delicate balance between planning for the demands of the individual and those of the group.

## Ground Work

For almost six decades Eckbo gave form to our social landscape. He continuously framed his theories and social ideals within the search for a modern idiom, establishing a perpetual dialogue among people, nature, and aesthetics. With his Harvard fellows Dan Kiley and James Rose, Eckbo published articles that stressed the necessity for a revised approach to landscape design, whether for an urban, rural, or primeval situation. Echoing Christopher Tunnard, the triumvirate of modernist graduate students argued for the application of science to the field of landscape design and for the use of vegetation sculpturally, if not structurally. As if to announce Tunnard's 1942 claim that the "right style for the twentieth century is no style at all, but a new conception of planning the human environment," Eckbo repeatedly stated the irrelevance of style to landscape design.[3] Instead of deepening the schism between formal and informal styles, he asserted, one should seek a dual understanding of biology and geometry. Abandoning the classical references of his early student investigations, such as An Estate in the Manner of Louis XIV designed while at Berkeley [see figure 2], Eckbo's Harvard projects veered decisively toward modernism. The 1937 Freeform Park was a "Memorial to the Fathers of our Country" situated on Potomac Island, where the informal became modern, and the modern went informal [see figures 10–11; plate I]. If the circulation and general geometries of Freeform Park still retained a traditional structure reminiscent of Fletcher

**83**
Flexible Co-op (project).
Circa 1945.
The adjustable screens facilitated the transformation of private space into public.
[*Documents Collection*]

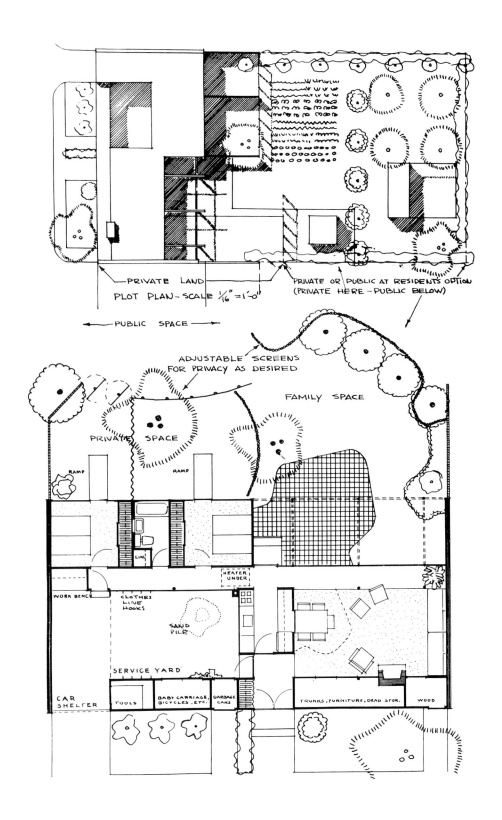

PRIVATE LAND

PLOT PLAN-SCALE ⅟₁₆"=1'-0"

PRIVATE OR PUBLIC AT RESIDENT'S OPTION
(PRIVATE HERE - PUBLIC BELOW)

◄— PUBLIC SPACE —►

ADJUSTABLE SCREENS
FOR PRIVACY AS DESIRED

FAMILY SPACE

PRIVATE SPACE

RAMP

RAMP

LIN

HEATER
UNDER

WORK BENCH

CLOTHES
LINE
HOOKS

SAND
PILE

SERVICE YARD

CAR
SHELTER

TOOLS

BABY CARRIAGE,
BICYCLES, ETC.

GARBAGE
CANS

TRUNKS, FURNITURE, DEAD STOR.

WOOD

Steele's classical modernity, two of Eckbo's later student projects clearly departed from such references.

For the 1937 Small Gardens in the City, Eckbo shaped the backyards of an entire urban block [see figures 21, 22a-d]. Although he designed most of the gardens as individual entities, the play of partition walls affecting two neighboring lots announced his future explorations in site planning. The postwar Flexible Co-op project, for instance, structured the garden in gradients of privacy: as one moved away from the house, the space remained private or became semi-public through the manipulation of boundaries — hedges and movable screens [figure 83].

Eckbo's thesis project, Contempoville, also studied the formal variations of individual residential gardens but added a public dimension with a central communal open space [figure 84]. His proposal situated Contempoville in Los Angeles, at the time of a hypothetical 1945 world's fair, which would have "portray[ed] the World of Day-After-Tomorrow [through] an exposition of the most advanced design-thought of the day." To answer the wishes of his client, Eckbo developed a block of model suburban homes composed of twenty-three houses, whose plans he borrowed from contemporary architectural magazines, placed on half-acre lots around a ten-acre park. The park offered "active recreational facilities" for residents of all ages, thereby leaving money and space for a "more pleasing landscape development" of individual lots.[4] The garden plans were extremely varied but consistent in the modernity of their idioms [see figure 23]. Arp-inspired biomorphic shapes, replicas of Legrain's zigzag lawn border [see figure 13], and explosions of angled lines shaped the ground plane. Similarly, enclosing elements and sylvan architecture manipulated the spatial envelope. By alternating translucent and opaque walls, and hedges above and below eye-level, Eckbo confused the sense of boundary and implied a continuation of the dynamically layered space into the depth of the park. A caption read: "Beginning with geometrical lot lines and house forms, shrubs and trees are placed in a consciously ordered arrangement to control the garden space. However, nature will dominate these gardens, because the plant material is so placed that it can continue its growth with a minimum of interference by the hand of man."[5] Such divorcing of the graphic ground plane from the vegetal mass foreshadowed Eckbo's landscape

*The Fair Committee expects good, clean, intelligent contemporary design, nothing "modernistic," cheap, or "expositiony." The exhibit is expected to express the best of contemporary life, and to suggest a mould for the higher development of future life. The project is not considered as of sufficient scale to become an example of town planning. It is rather an exhibition of the best middle-class residential design, obtained through close and sympathetic collaboration of the best architectural and landscape design talent.*

[from Garrett Eckbo, thesis program statement, 15 February 1938]

**84**

Contempoville: A Model Block of Suburban Homes, to be exhibited at the Los Angeles 1945 World's Fair. Site plan. Thesis project, Harvard University, 1938.

[*Documents Collection*]

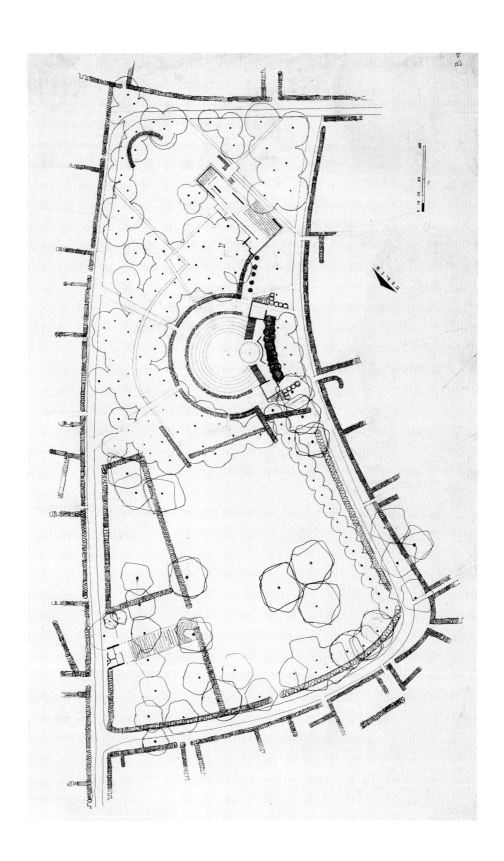

compositions for the migrant camps, as well as his planned communities in southern California, where the volumetrically varied plantings effaced the rigor of their arrangement.

The communal amenities of Contempoville included an outdoor theater, children's playgrounds, tennis court, swimming pool, and its shelter [figure 85]. Centrally placed within the block, these were arranged inside groves of trees and partitions of hedges. For the pool shelter, the landscape architect borrowed Ludwig Mies van der Rohe's 1929 Barcelona Pavilion [see figure 25], which—in Eckbo's own words—had thus "achieved (or descended to) functional community use."[6] If the transformation of this icon of modernist architecture—witnessed in the revision of the reflecting pool into a swimming pool—may seem irreverent to some, the homage to Mies was genuine. Seeking the concept of house-and-garden as an organic unit, Eckbo cited contemporary architecture for what he termed "decentralized building and open space arrangements, in which one can find no façades."[7] He translated Mies's depth-enhancing overlay of architectonic planes into shifting hedges that suggested unbounded space within the scale of the private garden. Although Eckbo later dismissed Contempoville as falling short of being a community— qualifying his student thinking, not in social or planning terms, but exclusively in formal terms—this project held all the promise of his future investigations in site space design and social involvement.[8]

Formally, Mies van der Rohe's dissolving of the architectural envelope would find literal applications in several of the public landscapes Eckbo conceived just after graduation [figure 86]. He spent half of 1938 in Washington, D.C., designing guideline schemes for public housing recreation spaces at the request of Frederick Gutheim (assistant information director, United States Housing Authority).[9] In these theoretical projects, the vocabulary of Contempoville was further developed, as well as simplified. The shifting and overlapping of planes —hedges and screens, benches, pools, and sandboxes—and architectonic rows of trees defined various use areas, whose rigor was softened by the curvilinear wrappings of grassed islands and tree canopies. Plantings were minimal, to reduce maintenance. Untrimmed hedges partially reinforced the edges of the central space and established a link with the tenant yards. These vegetal screens framed the "free play," "quiet," "shelter," or "apparatus" zones. Regulated by allées

**85**
Contempoville. Central park with shelter (replica of the 1929 Barcelona [German] Pavilion), outdoor theater, and playgrounds. Plan. Thesis project, Harvard University, 1938.
[*Documents Collection*]

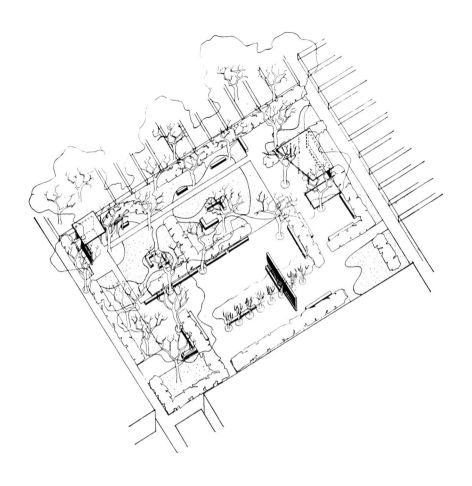

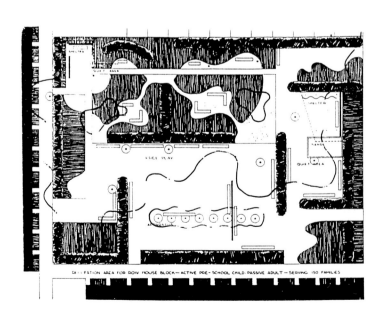

RECREATION AREA FOR ROW HOUSE BLOCK — ACTIVE PRE-SCHOOL CHILD PASSIVE ADULT — SERVING 150 FAMILIES

and bosks (which were "transparent," that is not fully blocking the view), architectural partitions (above and below eye level), and hedges (opaque, blocking the view), the space was varied, yet neither confining nor labyrinthine, and thus offered the ideal terrain for the "active pre-school child."[10]

Although Eckbo came from a modest background and had been exposed by osmosis at Harvard to the social ethos of European modernism — in courses offered by Walter Gropius and Marcel Breuer — his student years were relatively sheltered from the effects of the depression. Upon his return to the San Francisco Bay Area, however, Eckbo immersed himself in one of the major enterprises of federal relief planning, when he joined the Farm Security Administration (FSA) in 1939.

## A New Deal

*The nomads had been the followers of flocks and herds,*
*Or the wilder men, the hunters, the raiders.*
*The harvesters had been the men of homes.*

*But ours is a land of nomad harvesters.*[11]

Early in his presidency, Franklin Delano Roosevelt advocated the need for national planning as a palliative to the economic freefall that followed the 1929 Wall Street crash and plagued individuals across the country [figure 87].[12] Planning policies were drafted to establish rural communities that would offer advantages equal to those of urban settlements; to create new towns in undeveloped areas; and to reform land-use and agricultural economic patterns.[13] Ironically, the centralized bureaucracy promoted the most advanced planning ideals through the actions of visionary individuals, as it was forced by stringent time constraints to decentralize, thus relinquishing power and control.

Initiated by the Division of Subsistence Homesteads in the Department of the Interior and the Federal Emergency Relief Administration at the outset of Roosevelt's first term, communities were later developed by the Resettlement Administration (RA) and finally by the Farm Security Administration [figure 88]. With roots in the socialist theories of Charles Fourier and Robert Owen, the American rural cooperative models of the 1930s further reinforced the back-to-the-land movement initiated at the beginning of the century.

**86**
Study for public housing recreation areas. Axonometric drawing and plan.
Designed for the United States Housing Authority. Washington D.C., 1938.
[*Courtesy Garrett Eckbo*]

This movement had advertised the financial advantages of returning to an agrarian economy in opposition to the evils of industrialization. After the 1929 crash, however, it was the quest for survival rather than better economic prospects that drove hordes of back-to-the-landers out of cities. In his inaugural speech on 4 March 1933, Roosevelt urged Americans to "recognize the overbalance of population in industrial centers and, by engaging on a national scale in a redistribution, endeavor to provide a better use of the land for those best fitted for the land."[14] Eckbo would later denounce this type of sentimentalism while he agreed with the need for the specificity of design standards applied to rural situations.[15]

On 30 April 1935 Roosevelt placed Rexford Tugwell at the helm of the newly created Resettlement Administration, whose goals included establishing communities for destitute or low-income families in rural and suburban areas. Other charges concerned reforestation, erosion control, flood control, rural rehabilitation, and recreational development. We need only review the legacy left across America by New Deal programs such as the Civilian Conservation Corps (CCC), the Works Progress Administration (WPA), the Soil Conservation Service (SCS), or the Tennessee Valley Authority (TVA) to understand the value of federal planning in the development of public domain. It was the hopelessness of the depression that had both instigated and permitted the intervention of the federal government. By the second half of the 1930s, however, with the likely prospect of future economic recovery, the assisted population showed less tolerance toward the somewhat paternalistic directives of the planned communities. The Resettlement Administration, and later the Farm Security Administration, would pursue relief as well as permanent reform. The RA's ambitious mission was caustically described by a journalist as attempting "to rearrange the earth and the people thereof and devote surplus time and money, if any, to a rehabilitation of the Solar System."[16] Even the basic relief of migratory camps was met with loud protests from the growers, who feared that the concentration of a semi-permanent labor force would permit organization.[17] Thus large-scale farmers and farm organizations hardly viewed the system of grants and loans that allowed individual farmers and cooperatives to gain ownership of land as a necessity. Both relief administrations would be vilified by powerful agricultural lobbies as harboring Communist tendencies.

Jeremy looked up. Fifty yards ahead, an ancient Ford was creeping tremulously along the road. It carried, lashed insecurely to roof and running boards and luggage rack, a squalid cargo of household goods – rolls of bedding, an old iron stove, a crate of pots and pans, a folded tent, a tin bath.... "Transients," the chauffeur explained in a tone of contempt. "What's that?" Jeremy asked. "Why, transients," the negro repeated, as though the emphasis were an explanation." Guess that lot's from the dust bowl. Kansas license plate. Come to pick our navels." "Come to pick your navels?" Jeremy echoed incredulously. "Navel oranges," said the chauffeur. "It's the season. Pretty good year for navels, I guess."
[from Aldous Huxley, After Many a Summer Dies the Swan, 1939]

87
"Typical of thousands of migrating agricultural laborers. California. March, 1937."
[Dorothea Lange, courtesy Bancroft Library, University of California at Berkeley]

88
Tulare Camp. Aerial view. Tulare Basin, San Joaquin Valley, 1937–42. Farm Security Administration.
[from Pencil Points]

The National Labor Relations Act, signed into law by Roosevelt in July 1935, precluded agricultural laborers from the rights and protections guaranteed to industrial workers. The westward displacement of farmers from the southcentral states — Oklahoma and Arkansas in particular — exacerbated the meager conditions of the rural caste and brought the New Deal Administration and its emergency relief programs to the field of migrant housing and health. Forced off their farms, hundreds of thousands of refugees from the so-called Dust Bowl flowed into California. The field reports prepared by the econ-omist Paul Taylor and illustrated by Dorothea Lange's photographs publicized the plight of white migrant workers and shocked an America that had otherwise remained oblivious to the equally unfor-tunate working and living conditions of Mexican, Asian, or black labor-ers.[18] Settling mostly in the Central Valley, the new wave of temp-farmers lived along roads, in private labor camps, overcrowded auto and trailer camps, shack towns, and squatter camps [figure 89]. With Tugwell's resignation, the controversial Resettlement Administration was reborn in September 1937 under the guise of the Farm Security Administration, with Will Alexander at its head. The new agency carried on the work and planning ventures of the Resettlement Administration, placing an emphasis on the aid to the lowest stratum

of farmers, found in the migrant laborers of California and the Southern sharecroppers.[19]

Perhaps in reaction to the criticism of Tugwell's excessive power and control, the twelve regional offices of the FSA operated independently of the parent agency in Washington on all matters except final approval of designs and cost. This lack of bureaucratic interference paired with an absence of precedent allowed the regional offices to act locally and experiment with architectural and landscape design, site planning, and engineering. Talbot Hamlin, tireless proselytizer for modern American architecture, described the FSA communities as "human and attractive because their designers understood people and their needs, and insisted that all those needs—intellectual and emotional as well as physical—should be taken care of. They are beautiful because designed by artists, to whom creation was not limited by any economic deadline and to whom it was as necessary to think in creative form terms of a privy as of a community center."[20]

The planning production of the San Francisco FSA office was somewhat codified: hexagon-shaped camps in California (Tulare) as well as in Arizona (Eleven-Mile Corner); modernist prisms of multi-family units in adobe were erected at Chandler, Arizona, and in wood and

**89**
A Hooverville.
*[Dorothea Lange, courtesy Bancroft Library, University of California at Berkeley]*

**90**
Chandler Co-operative Farm housing. Southwest garden facade (oriented toward prevailing breezes). Arizona, 1936–37, 1939. Farm Security Administration.
*[Courtesy Garrett Eckbo]*

composition board at Yuba City, Tulare, and Taft in California [figures 90–92]. This rationalized planning addressed a typical function — the relief of day farmers and their families. Atypical, however, were the time frame of construction and life span of these facilities. Intended as emergency solutions to a temporary crisis, they were conceived as instant towns that would probably never mature and whose surreal character must have rivaled that of movie sets propped up in the middle of the desert.

Ironically, the social underpinning of the FSA venture, at least for the San Francisco office, generated an approach to architecture whose formal stance would be recognized internationally. Thus the cooperative farm of Chandler, for example, which Vernon DeMars and Burton Cairns planned and designed, was selected as one of the two examples of American modern architecture to illustrate Alfred Roth's *Die Neue Architektur 1930–1940*.[21] Roth duly highlighted the design's response to climatic and functional constraints: the housing units were set at an angle to the road and at a right angle to the prevailing winds, so as to maximize their cooling capabilities. Adobe offered thermal advantages; its labor-intensive, self-help construction process provided work for the unemployed; and its traditional roots tied the buildings to the vernacular. The lower units were shaded by the first floor overhang, itself protected from direct sunlight by a protruding roof.

Roth also recorded the various landscape additions to this flat site, which before agricultural irrigation "was a cactus-covered desert." The kitchen-dining room extended outward, into the individual garden, under the shade of a poplar (albeit a strange choice for a shade tree). The garden was designed almost as if it belonged to a standard urban lot, in its elongated dimensions as well as in its features. The "sitting out place" was bounded by hedges, fragrant with herbs, and decorated with geranium, morning glory, and rockrose; the clothesline ruled over the lawn patch and a fruit tree marked the limits of the lot. Such mundane — yet elegant — arrangements revealed the importance of landscape as a common denominator within a wide spectrum of cultural origins. Everybody everywhere needed a tree, especially when "everywhere" was not home. Thus vegetation acted as an anchor to the land. It was both universal and traditional. Because of such features, Eckbo's efforts to create an indigenous

**91**
Tulare Camp.
Aerial view of multi-family housing units, with trailer camp in the background. Tulare Basin, San Joaquin Valley, 1937–42. Farm Security Administration.
[*Courtesy Garrett Eckbo*]

**92**
Taft Defense Housing. San Joaquin Valley, 1941. Farm Security Administration.
[*Courtesy Garrett Eckbo*]

and formally innovative lexicon for the migrant camps were particularly noteworthy.

## A New Landscape Deal

Eckbo held one of the positions of landscape architect at the San Francisco FSA office (Regions IX and XI) from 1939 until 1942. Vernon DeMars became acting district architect, after the death of Burton Cairns; Herbert Hallsteen was district engineer and Nicholas Cirino, regional engineer. Their official goal was to design the physical framework for shelter, sanitation, education, and care for migrant workers across the western states. The majority of these camps were established in California, which, with its extensive mechanized agriculture and the vast influx of migrant laborers, required the most intensive relief efforts. Thus, the San Francisco office planned communities for Ceres, Gridley, Winters, Thornton, Westley, Firebaugh, Mineral King, Tulare, Shafter, Arvin, Brawley, Marysville, Yuba City, and Coachella. Other sites included Walla Walla, Granger, and Yakima in Washington; Yamhill in Oregon; Caldwell and Twin Falls in Idaho; Yuma, Glendale, Agua Fria, Chandler, Casa Grande, Eleven-Mile Corner, and Baxter in Arizona; Weslaco, Harlingen, Robstown, and Sinton in Texas. As a norm across the states, landscape design concentrated on providing

**93**
Shafter Camp.
Tents on platforms with trellis extensions.
Tulare Basin, San Joaquin Valley, 1938.
Farm Security Administration.

[*The Dorothea Lange Collection, The Oakland Museum of California, The City of Oakland.*]

shade, preventing erosion and dust, and ultimately — to cite Eckbo — expanding and framing the architecture.[22]

Economic, social, and climatic factors determined the planning of home, trailer, and tent communities for permanent, semi-permanent, and transient residents [figure 93]. The permanent section of the camps housed between one and three hundred occupants; the temporary areas needed to accommodate up to a thousand migrants, who lived in metal shelters — usually replacing the platform-tent units of the early camps — or trailers. The transients' area of the camp was arranged in a linear block pattern, hexagons, or double hexagons, to allow continuity of circulation within controlled borders. In contrast, the permanent residents lived in individual houses or multi-family housing that formed distinct neighborhoods. The site plans usually organized the homes in cul-de-sac pattern and staggered the one- or two-story apartment units to idealize orientation to sun and wind and to ensure privacy. The inhabitants of both houses and apartments maintained private subsistence plots. The park, sports, and recreational facilities complemented the community buildings, usually located close to the temporary residents' lodgings, where the demand for such amenities was greater [figure 94].[23]

**94**
Tulare Unit; central open space for the trailer camp. Site plan. Tulare Basin, San Joaquin Valley, 1937–42. Farm Security Administration. The assembly hall is at the right of plan with the utility building at left.
[Documents Collection]

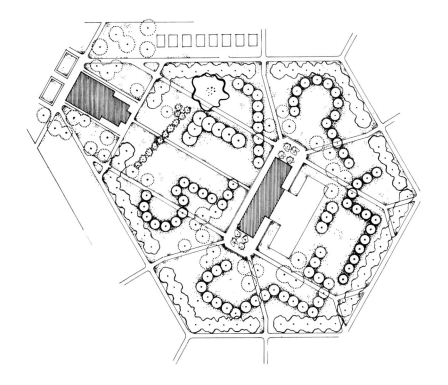

During his FSA years Eckbo experimented with what he termed the "assembly-line-technique" of modern site planning. Site planning integrated all aspects of design, a means to approach the expansive as well as the restrictive nature of landscape. He wrote that comprehensive study was needed to determine the best possible relationships among buildings, utilities, recreation facilities, planting, and open space. Thus, cohesive site planning, regardless of scale should be the "arrangement of environments for people." Its ultimate goal was to "produce the best possible physical pattern within which a group of people can develop a good social pattern."[24] Eckbo described gardens as forming spaces in which the structural elements of ground plane, enclosure, and canopy were interdependent and equally important.[25] But ultimately, the raison d'être of landscape design was to provide a setting for human activity, and the migrant camps were no exception.

The creation of diverse outdoor spaces defined with enclosures of varying heights and density — paired with amenities — fostered social exchange, during "free play" or games of baseball, in hanging laundry or dancing [figure 95]. The park, addressing the community building, served as an outdoor extension for the functions taking place inside — shaded and sheltered from the wind — and as the common green for the garden-less trailers surrounding it and for the colony as a whole. With the active practice of religion officially discouraged by the camp's "constitution," recreational activities would provide the arena for communal interaction.

As Eckbo observed in his article on design in the rural environment, the grouping of agricultural communities offered social and recreational advantages as well as those of cooperative economy: "whereas in the cities the need is for *more free space* (decentralization)," he wrote, "the rural need is for *more intensive use of less space* (concentration)."[26] The frontier model of the homesteader — in which the family stood as both the social and the recreational unit — needed revision. So did rural housing and rural recreation. The expansion of territory and scattering of population that characterized the industrialization of agriculture made social contact more essential than ever. Productivity may be a key element in the organization of a rural area, wrote Eckbo, but it still should rely on the understanding of the physical as well as cultural aspects of that area. Hence the need to grasp

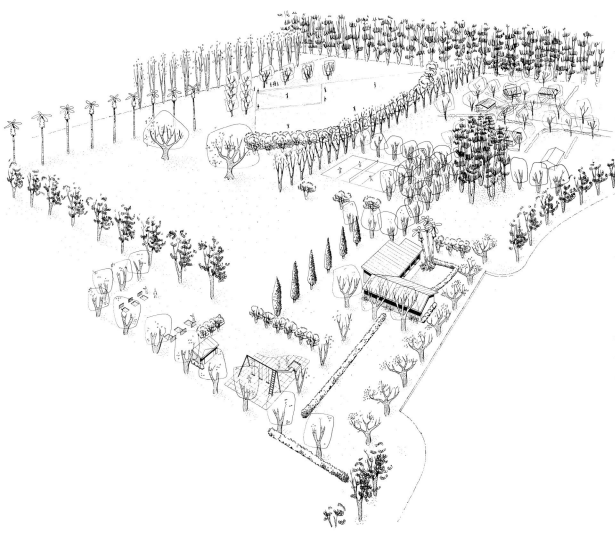

**95**

Ceres Camp.
Community recreation
space. San Joaquin Valley,
1940. Farm Security
Administration.
"Large tree patterns at the
baroque scale of cheap
rural land."

[*Documents Collection*]

the importance of a well developed local road network, in addition to the interstate highway system, of grouped rural housing, and of organized recreation.

Rural recreation may be too novel a field to have established standards, Eckbo continued, but its facilities should foster group activities and competition, including concerts, dance, sports, and drama. But standards did exist, as evidenced by the three-volume *Park and Recreation Structures* published by the National Park Service in 1938. Formally, these campsites and facilities had little in common with Eckbo's take on the rural landscape — as they complemented forested natural beauties with rustic buildings and campfire circles. Furthermore, their aim also differed, in that the National Park tent and trailer campsites accommodated voluntary, and most likely urban, dwellers and not agricultural refugees. Despite their rather pastoral image, the National Parks exerted some form of control as "the tent camper seem[ed] to exercise (and to get away with!) an inversion of the right of eminent domain. He [held] any attempt to regulate his tenancy and conduct in the public interest to be ultra vires and inhibiting of his ruggedly individualistic prerogatives."[27] It was this very rugged individualism — generally associated with the frontier spirit of farmers — that appears to have warranted the strict arrangement, the supervising administration, and constitution of the FSA settlements. Instead of a layout of cabins, dining lodges, craft shops, and wash houses scattered amidst groves of trees by the Civilian Conservation Corps, the architecture and landscape architecture team of the San Francisco FSA office favored a highly hierarchical plan more akin to the Renaissance new town than to any "delightful informality" so scorned by Eckbo. The latter considered that "we may as well accept the fact that man's activities change and dominate the landscape," although adding, "it does not follow that they should spoil it."[28] Thus he would look toward the ordered patterns of agriculture as theaters for, and models of, design interventions.

Eckbo stated once again his sympathy for a formed landscape, arguing that the "romantic informality" of the countryside was a concept that had long needed overhauling; agricultural fields did not "'blend' with nature" but instead showed human organization of nature. Then, he concluded, "whence… the theory that landscape and building design must go rustic in the rural areas."[29] To sustain his argument, he utilized the modernist architecture of the FSA camps as a possible model for rural housing. Part-time farm colonies that promoted sustainability, such as Chandler, had an edge over the camp dependent on, and an appendage to, the agricultural industry — a trend Carey McWilliams saw as encouraging, if only as a signpost on the road to reform. To McWilliams,

> the real solution involves the substitution of collective agriculture for the present monopolistically owned and controlled system…. A partial solution will be achieved when subsistence homesteads have grown up about the migratory camps…. It is just possible that [the] latest recruits for the farm factories may be the last, and that out of their struggle for a decent life in California may issue a new type of agricultural economy for the West and for America.[30]

The FSA did attempt to stabilize migration patterns within various states. The highly specialized agricultural industry tended to employ a large seasonal labor force that rural communities could not absorb year-round. The relief administration thus experimented with variable-geometry or variable-demography settlements whose plans evolved from sports fields and vice versa. The camp of Woodville, located among the cotton, grapes, asparagus, and citrus fields of the lower San Joaquin Valley of California, was planned as the nucleus of a new small town. The aim was to retire the camp as the seasonal users were replaced with permanent residents — should additional employment arise. Located on a flat bare site, Woodville was praised by architectural critics for the quality of its planning as well as for the design of its community buildings [figure 96].[31] The arrangement balanced the temporary metal shelters with single and row houses that recalled those erected at Yuba City. Lavatory, laundry, and shower facilities served the migrant residents — constituting three-quarters of Woodville's population — while the co-op store, school, and community building joined camp and "town" areas. The tri-alar school and community building was a lesson in economy and flexibility: low prisms linked by exterior corridors opened the various classrooms directly to agricultural fields and orchards; with the assembly room

doubling as the school gymnasium, the complex furnished "areas for child instruction, adult instruction, recreation, and social gatherings, adjustable to almost any use."[32]

Elizabeth Mock, curator of Architecture and Design at New York's Museum of Modern Art, assessed Woodville's "handsome buildings [as] the result of careful and economical design: FSA's San Francisco office has shown that 'bureaucratic architecture' can also be distinguished."[33] The placement of the gatehouse beyond the center and homes area, "in control of the camp section only," so as "to remove any suggestion of a Government reservation," was perhaps an indicator of the social hierarchy within the settlement itself.[34] In their time-axis conception, such camps reflected similar patterns as those of immigration, for example, the recent arrivals pushing the lower strata upward.[35]

To complement such "touch[es] of European modern [architecture] in the western landscape," Eckbo sought an optimal structuring of outdoor spaces with planting patterns that were distinctly his own [figure 97].[36] At Weslaco, Texas, he designed a dozen variations for the park addressing the gatehouse and garage with modifications of the "grass-shrub-tree relationship."[37] All schemes, modular yet varied, bore a close resemblance to modern art, with formal manipulations of green elements — lines, arcs, and free forms [figures 98–99]. With outdoor rooms, suggestions of enclosure, and rhythmic punctuations of spaces, Eckbo followed the dictum of "blocking off portions so there is a succession of views and to set up movement and circulation."[38]

Throughout his landscapes, he formed space by arranging the elements of surfacing, enclosure, and "enrichment" — that is "pictures, 'compositions,' patterns [and] flower borders." With "enrichment" limited by economic or practical constraints, his equation relied on the possibilities offered by "sensitive and imaginative selection and arrangement of enclosure and surfacing elements." He saw this option as "equally satisfying with no more than the greatest enrichment of all — human life and activity."

Eckbo frequently asserted that open space should be considered the skeleton and controlling form of the site plan, rather than the by-

**96**
Woodville school and community center.
Aerial perspective.
Tulare Basin, San Joaquin Valley, 1941.
Farm Security Administration.
[Courtesy Garrett Eckbo]

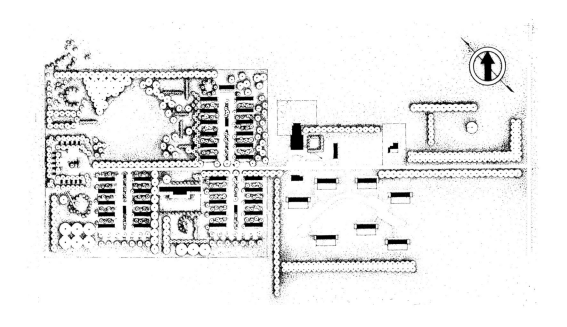

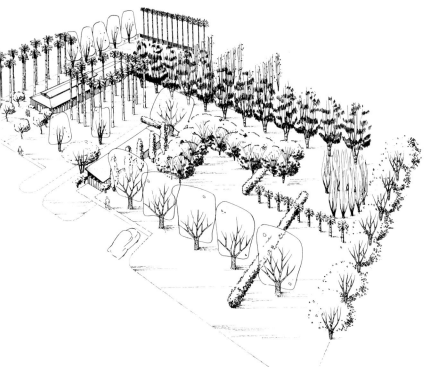

**97**

Weslaco Unit. Site plan.
Texas, 1939. Farm Security
Administration. Photostat.
Buildings in upper center
frame the site of Eckbo's
alternate park schemes,
shown at left and
opposite.

[*Documents Collection*]

**98**

Weslaco Unit.
Park for community build-
ing and gatehouse / garage.
Aerial perspective. Texas,
1939. Farm Security
Administration.
Ink on tracing paper.

[*Documents Collection*]

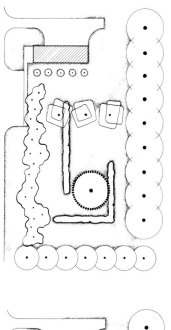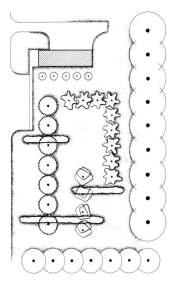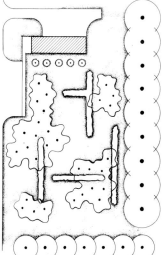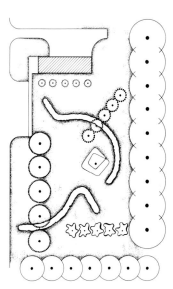

**99**

Weslaco Unit. Park for
gatehouse / garage. Four of
twelve plan variations.
Texas, 1939. Farm Security
Administration.
Ink on tracing paper.
[*Documents Collection*]

These studies indicate
"the potential variety of
grass-shrub-tree relations
which can be developed
beyond the standard
interpretation of meadow."
[*from Garrett Eckbo*,
Landscape for Living]

product of the buildings arrangement and roadways.[39] As he entered the FSA office relatively late in the operation of the program, however, his major planning investigations were directed toward the design of the parks for permanent homes rather than the overall layout of camps [figure 100]. Built on federal land, the settlements were beyond the control or harassment of state and county agencies, and by private militias. Intended to protect — if not isolate — the residents from the environment and social tensions, the camp design attempted to create a climatic haven and a sense of place for the transients. To counter the aridity and heat of the California valleys, Texas, or Arizona, Eckbo used plantings as shelter and as the spatial structure for life and play [figure 101]. Tree canopies or trellises countered the sun or functioned as outdoor rooms complementing the tent, trailer, or housing units. The allées, screens, and clusters of vegetation defined specific spaces assigned to specific functions: roads, drying yards, common play areas, or individual vegetable gardens. Praising the designs the San Francisco office produced for the migrant workers, the architectural critic Talbot Hamlin hardly commented on the formal landscape improvements, but he remarked on the attention given to, and the necessity for, vegetation:

> In all of this site planning the problem has been seen as a human and as an aesthetic problem as well as a problem in serving practical ends. Thus the most careful use has been made of existing trees, and where definite groves or stands of timber exist on the property these areas have been chosen wherever possible for the community buildings, the schools and the more permanent houses, so that the migrant driving in dusty after a day's work in blazing shadeless field or a long run over sunbeaten and windswept highways may find his relaxation in a place dappled with leaf shadows, embowered with trees and with the heartening feel of green and growing things around. Moreover, tree planting and a certain amount of modest landscaping has formed an essential part of all the communities.[40]

The site plan of the camp at Taft favored a centripetal arrangement in which the two-story units not only sought the best orientation but also formed a visual closure that served as a "sheltered oasis" [figure 102]. Heavy plantings of hardy species such as black locust, Siberian

**100**
Mineral King Co-operative Ranch. Community park. Aerial perspective. Near Visalia, Tulare Basin, San Joaquin Valley, 1939. Farm Security Administration. Ink on tracing paper. [*Documents Collection*]

**101**
Shafter Unit. Shelter/play structure. Tulare Basin, San Joaquin Valley, 1937–41. Farm Security Administration. Note the combination trellis/bench/sandbox. [*Courtesy Garrett Eckbo*]

elm, and coast beefwood withstood the extreme temperature range and dry climate of the San Joaquin Valley and structured the landscape scheme.[41] Highly tolerant of wind, drought, and poor soil conditions, these trees were also extremely fast-growing if irrigated. Such perfect subjects for soil conservation or land reclamation fought wind erosion by providing excellent windbreaks and shelter belts. In addition to creating express landscapes in deserts, Eckbo also relied on, or supplemented, vegetation present on the site. His interventions could be thus defined as either *adaptations*, the creation of oases within the harsh environment; *insertions*, when he complemented the landscape with a reinforcing vegetal structure; or *appropriations*, when he integrated entire groves of existing trees to his scheme [figures 103–4]. The planting plan of Winters, west of Sacramento, combined the latter two modes, as Eckbo laid out the Farm Labor Homes within apricot and walnut orchards and subverted their formal order with hedges, groves, and lines of hackberry, Chinese pistachio, and Chinese elm.

Eckbo described plantings not only as providing shade, greenery, color, and general amenity but also as the final refining element in the complete spatial design of the site. The landscape architect should collaborate with the architect and the engineer on site planning from the very beginning, wrote Eckbo, "if he is to be saved from the fate of being an exterior decorator for architecture. The keynote of the planting scheme should be the use of plants as space-organizing elements rather than as decoration."[42] Spines of trees offered protection from wind while enclosing spaces such as baseball fields or other play areas, reinforcing circulation patterns, and implying movement. Lines of shrubs also outlined outdoor rooms and multiplied viewpoints, thereby suggesting a continuation of space beyond the actual boundaries of the park.

For inspiration, Eckbo saw no better source than the rural landscape itself — the congruence of people and nature.

> [With] innumerable definite three-dimensional space forms produced with both structural and natural materials: rectangular or polygonal fields cut from solid natural wildwoods; trees in rows or belts forming planes; the regularity of orchards; straight lines of

**102**
Taft Defense Housing. Central open space. San Joaquin Valley, 1941. Farm Security Administration.
[*Courtesy Garrett Eckbo*]

**103**
Yuba City Unit. Aerial view. Sacramento Valley, 1937–39. Farm Security Administration. Housing for permanent residents surrounds a grove of existing trees, in the foreground, with the double hexagon of the migrant workers' trailer camp beyond.
[*from* Architectural Forum]

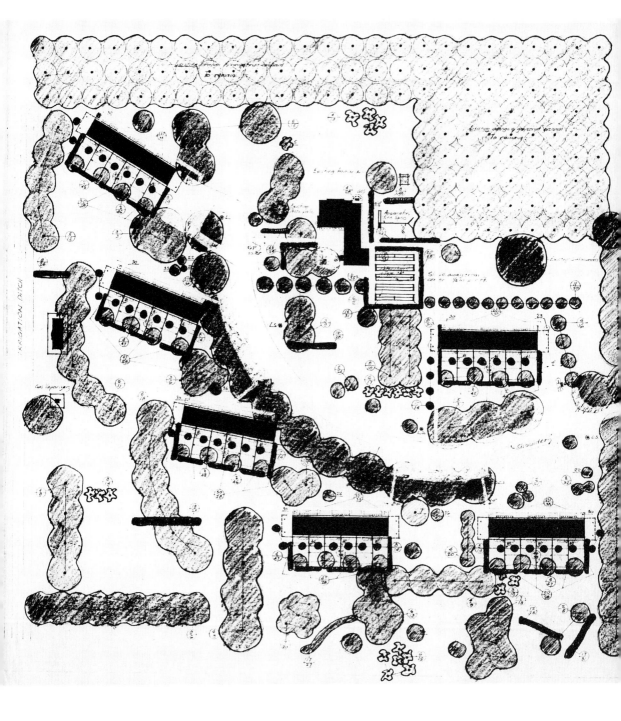

*untrimmed hedges and mixed hedgerows...; free-standing clumps*
*of trees forming natural pavilions; intersecting planes of these*
*lines of trees and hedges and walls forming a fragmentary orga-*
*nization of space. It is seldom completely enclosed; always there*
*is a suggestion of its continuity, something to follow, the stimulat-*
*ing impossibility of seeing all of the space at once.*[43]

The landscape design of the Shafter camp appeared as an interpretation of the standard agricultural fields [figure 105–6].[44] Each of the
twenty-nine permanent home lots was sufficiently large to raise subsistence crops, a majority of indigenous trees structured the two-acre
park, and in the play areas, the "light frame trellis-and-screen structures [stood as] abstractions of typical practical agricultural crop
structures." Despite the stringent budget, Eckbo accorded great
attention to the spatial definition of house and circulation areas.
Announcing the later vegetation codings of postwar projects such as
Community Homes, he drew three site plans keyed accordingly to
the height of trees and shrubs.

The camps were located strategically along the migratory routes
followed by laborers, and within proximity of employment, which
allowed Eckbo to take advantage of the extremely rich soil of the
Californian agricultural valleys. And being of the opinion that "it has
yet to be proven that long plant lists necessarily increase costs," he
planted heavily and variedly.[45] He sought to create "large tree patterns at the baroque scale on cheap rural land," using eucalyptus,
palm tree, and poplar as the backbone of the layout; oak, olive tree,
and magnolia to offer shade; and almond and plum trees for color
[figure 107].[46] Thus the geometries that looked rigidly systematic in
plan were offset in reality by the variegation of trees and shrubs.
This sampling of vegetation could be seen as reminiscent of the gardens Eckbo designed for Armstrong Nurseries — a panoramic range
of species that softened the formality of the basic planting schemes
[see figures 5–7].

Although simple in manner, Eckbo's schemes for the FSA camps displayed a sophisticated spatial layering — both vertical and horizontal
— that recalled the formal variations of his theoretical Small Gardens
in the City of 1937. In the landscapes of relief, the lessons of modern
architecture were translated into planting designs where architec-

**104**
Yuma Unit; multi-family
housing. Site and planting
plan. Arizona, 1939. Farm
Security Administration.
Photostat.
*[Documents Collection]*

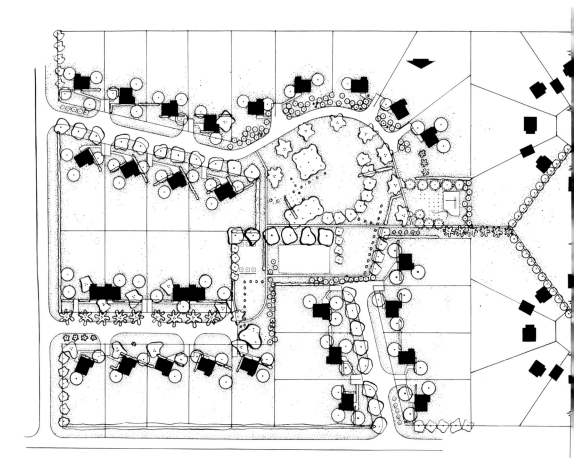

**105**

Shafter Unit; farm labor
homes for permanent
residents, with park.
Site plan. Tulare Basin,
San Joaquin Valley, 1941.
Farm Security
Administration.
Ink on tracing paper.
[*Documents Collection*]

**106**

Shafter Unit; farm labor
homes. Axonometric
drawing. Tulare Basin,
San Joaquin Valley, 1941.
Farm Security
Administration.
Ink and pencil on tracing
paper.
[*Documents Collection*]

**107**
Woodville.
The edge of row housing.
Tulare Basin,
San Joaquin Valley, 1941
Farm Security
Administration.

[*Courtesy Garrett Eckbo*]

tonic screens were enlarged through vegetation. And these designs, destined for the lowest-income group, shared the same formal investigations as those of his avant-garde private gardens: a rare instance of aesthetics at the service of the expedient.

The shaping of camps into the hexagons of ideal town plans transcribed an inner political order — with its own constitution and higher committee. It revealed an order that strove for humanism against the outside world and its Red-bashing militias.[47] To promote communities that instigated social as well as economic rehabilitation, the architects of the New Deal attempted to create a miniature society whose naïveté in pursuing a democratic and collective spirit was matched only by its fondness for keeping rural folklore. If the first Roosevelt administration had been placed under the sign of planning, the great depression era coincided with the idealization of regionalism. In times of economic and social uncertainty, the longing for a more secure past and a sense of place typically holds the promise of a recoverable order. Perhaps the designs of FSA camps best expressed the tug-of-war between reform and relief, progress and tradition. Their manufacturers put forward the social ideals of modernism — both in landscape and architecture — as a tool for stabilizing the human drift across the land. Such projects acted not only as design exhibits but also as social beacons, as Paul Conkin concluded in *Tomorrow a New World:*

> When a simple farmer, wide-eyed with wonder and expectancy… moved into a glittering new subsistence homesteads or resettlement community, he was entering a social show window. Willingly or unwillingly, knowingly or unknowingly, he was a human mannequin in a great exhibit, for the many architects of the New Deal communities, despite varying philosophies, were all striving to create, within the conducive environment of their planned villages, a new society, with altered values and new institutions.[48]

Eckbo's plantings evoked the order of, or sometimes borrowed from, the surrounding orchards; they also superimposed agrarian references and the indigenous with the forms of functionalism and exotic species. More often than not, however, Eckbo subverted the hermetic and controlling order of the camp. At Tulare, the hexagon-forming shelters addressed on one side the grid of an existing walnut orchard and on the other the central open space with its utilities building and assembly hall [figure 108]. The park itself appeared to draw more from patterns of paintings by László Moholoy-Nagy or Kasimir Malevich than from any rural precedent. The dynamic diffractions of space – with overlapping allées and green hemicycles — was enhanced by varied plantings. With the diverse scales and textures of tree of heaven, silver dollar gum, olive, camphor, and bottle tree, the eye of the hexagon seemed independent from the order of the camp. Within the trailer-bound ideal shape, Eckbo inserted another set of rules, just as formal but based on another geometry. Modifying the vertical scale and the degree of usual transparency between the patterns, he completely abolished any remnant of a Cartesian reading. Ultimately his order — totally alien to both surroundings and migrants — became the norm for the central spaces of many of the camps scattered across the west.

Urban, highly educated, secular young men oversaw the daily lives of rural, mostly non-educated, and frequently fundamentalist laborers from Arkansas and Oklahoma.[49] Similarly, in spite of Eckbo's claims that "*the country must be redesigned for country people* — i.e., neither from the viewpoint of nor for the benefit of the urbanite," his parks for the FSA were, most likely, alien to anything country people might have experienced before.[50] He did succeed in creating spatial identity — albeit architecturally derived, art-referential, and mostly highbrow — within the agrarian landscape of the West. His plantings, which appeared originally so diminutive when photographed next to the ready-made architecture of the camps, have now matured, and form ghost images of their social endeavor throughout the California valleys.

In spite of the higher ideal pursued in the creation of migrant camps — that of a new pattern of community life removed from an individualistic and materialistic society — the quantitative production of the FSA was deemed by many to be at best a stopgap solution. Not only did the sheer volume of exploited farm laborers living in squalor overwhelm the capabilities of the relief agency, but the assistance to migrants remained superficial rather than structural. The government-run camps functioned as a subsidy for farmers that relieved them of responsibility to provide housing or minimal wages.[51]

The results of such efforts, whose limited scope was perpetually threatened by agribusiness lobbies, are sadly summed up in today's migrant settlements, still inhabited by agricultural laborers — though of a different ethnicity [see plate II].[52] As Cletus Daniels concluded:

> Farmworkers in California were poor, uprooted, and powerless people long before Franklin Roosevelt's voice crackled over the radio imploring middle America to have courage in the face of depression and promising a new order of prosperity and economic justice in the days and years ahead. And they were no less poor, uprooted, and powerless after the reformist enthusiasm of the New Deal had waned and the attention of the nation had shifted from domestic to foreign affairs.[53]

## Emergency Landscapes

Between July 1940 and July 1943 at least three million workers had moved to sustain the ship, airplane, and munitions industries; with their families, the displaced masses totaled about seven million people.[54] They urgently required living accommodations. Name-brand architects contributing to the landscape of defense housing included Walter Gropius and Marcel Breuer, Eliel and Eero Saarinen, Buckminster Fuller, and more locally, William Wurster.[55] California's population increase made "the once famous *Grapes of Wrath* problem look like a picnic," stated the planning and housing expert Catherine Bauer.[56] Recognized for its efficient provision of emergency housing, the FSA had shifted its focus from migrant laborers' assistance to defense housing by 1941 [figure 109]. Eckbo served as landscape consultant for about fifty of these war housing projects. The socially and architecturally radical — and somewhat quixotic — efforts of the FSA era were definitely over as the government turned on its own. In 1942, before leaving the relief administration, Eckbo worked on developing camps for "Japanese evacuees" in the Owens Valley. His projects include the landscape plan for the staff housing section of Manzanar, a relocation unit for Japanese Americans. The camps of Marysville and Tulare originally destined for workers from the Dust Bowl, now served as temporary internment quarters.[57] Eckbo had joined the FSA to formulate a sheltering landscape for the displaced and landless; now

**108**

Tulare Unit. Site and planting plan, detail (12 December 1941). Tulare Basin, San Joaquin Valley. Farm Security Administration. Blueprint.

The shelters form a hexagon around the park; an existing walnut orchard lies between the migrant section and the permanent residents' homes.

[*Documents Collection*]

—however tragically—the relocation centers served as a mean of pure control, and instead of offering a sense of place reprieved from the outside world, they brought only a sense of isolation.

Eckbo had applied the lessons of high art, first advanced in the Contempoville project, to the basic functionalism of the FSA camps. In a similar way, he would learn from his experience with defense housing and trailer camps to establish a pattern for postwar suburban developments. As he would later write in *Landscape for Living*:

> The general theory is the grouping of the units in articulated cellular patterns in which the cells achieve special identity by virtue of the strong formal relations established within them. The total grouping achieves a spatial organization of the site with considerable movement and quality. Tree patterns and building colors can of course expedite this identifying articulation a great deal.[58]

Eckbo's contribution to FSA California war housing included the landscape plan for 72 units at Taft, designed by Vernon DeMars, and that for 3,000 single Navy workers and 200 families at Vallejo, with Theodore Bernardi and Vernon DeMars [figure 110]. Like Thomas Church's vegetal solutions for emergency landscapes, Eckbo's scheme for Vallejo attempted to provide neighborhood identity while relieving the rigidity of the matter-of-fact site plan. He relied on windbreak allées of Lombardy poplars and weeping willows to edge the various clusters of cabins, dormitories, restaurant, and administration buildings. He interspersed this formal order with specimen plantings of Japanese privet, sycamore, and *Pittosporum nigricans*, much as he had keyed the various areas of migrant camps with vegetation. The same ideal underlay FSA projects and war housing as "every technician involved in developing environments for people is responsible not just for providing shelter, but also for developing their fundamental potential dignity" [figure 111].[59]

Eckbo argued for planning defense housing without "the sacrifice of essential space to the twin bogeymen of cost and mechanical gadgetry, [nor] the vicious practise of developing minimum standards based on income strata, rather than optimum standards based on bio-ethnic needs," which he foresaw as "too apt to produce the slums of tomorrow."[60] In this deprecation of the Housing Authority's stan-

**109**
Defense housing trailer park. San Miguel, 1942. Farm Security Administration.

[*Courtesy Garrett Eckbo*]

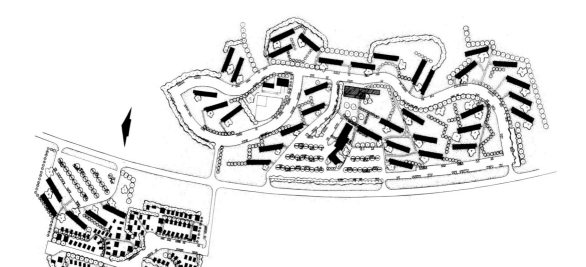

dards, he echoed Catherine Bauer's assertion that public housing and even more so, war housing, allotted too little space to both interiors and exteriors. This was a stance that Eckbo shared again, when he deemed that after the sacrifices of the war effort, Americans deserved, not minimum, but optimum standards in housing.

## A New Landscape for Living

Eckbo later recalled that no other project had given him as much satisfaction as designing landscapes for the migrant camps, resulting from the "combination of large open site without intensive demands beyond the already existing natural character and the social function." "As human density on the land increases," he continued, "demands for specific functions become more intensive. Trees, to survive at all, must be placed within (and enhancing) those functional patterns, rather than exploring those freer conceptions that [he] had dreamed of."[61] In spite of such reservations, functional constraints occasionally served design by reinforcing, and offering a foil to, Eckbo's space-defining plantings and "freer conceptions." In this regard, housing provided an essential driving force for his formal investigations.

In his postwar Flexible Co-op project, Eckbo conceived the house and garden as a whole. Individual privacy, family living, service elements, and public approach were integrated as indoor-outdoor sequences [see figure 83]. Privacy and views resulted from the planning of both the proximate and neighborhood contexts of the house. The optimum postwar standard of living required the planning of community facilities to parallel private amenities, much like the community building, parks, and public recreational facilities that complemented the homes and gardens of the FSA camps and the rural areas around them. In the Flexible Co-op project, group and child-care centers, neighborhood eating centers, laundry and shopping facilities reduced household drudgery, freeing women for more satisfying activities.[62]

In 1945 Eckbo collaborated on the site plan for the housing development of Ladera with Robert Royston and Nicholas Cirino — who had held the position of engineer for the FSA San Francisco office — and architects Joseph Allen Stein and John Funk, with whom he then shared an office [figure 112]. The founders of the

**110**
Defense housing "duration dormitories" and cabins for Navy yard workers. Site plan. Vallejo, 1942. Farm Security Administration. Tenant activities building seen in the upper segment of the site plan was designed by Bernardi, De Mars, Wickenden, Langhorst, and Funk.
[Documents Collection]

**111**
Defense housing dormitories. Sausalito, 1946.
[Courtesy Garrett Eckbo]

Peninsula Housing Association—who, like many postwar home builders, were disenchanted with typical suburban developments—had turned toward cooperative organization and the promise it held for an ideal democratic community.[63] The project distributed 400 single-family houses on a hilly 256-acre tract near Palo Alto, south of San Francisco. The plan called for an elementary school, kindergarten and playgrounds, gas station, guest house, and recreational, community, and commercial facilities. The shopping center was situated at the edge of the property in order to also serve surrounding developments, just as the community buildings of the migrant camps had served residents and neighboring farmers alike.

Balancing privacy and public amenities, the planning of Ladera echoed the recommendations of the Flexible Co-op project that demanded facilities for children, recreation, and shopping facilities. Broadly articulated by two through streets and a large wooded area, Ladera's overall plan laid out, along culs-de-sac, single lots that ranged between a quarter acre to two-and-a-half acres. In most instances, footpaths were segregated from vehicular traffic and residents could walk to park areas from almost anywhere in the subdivision without having to cross a through street. In addition to the existing clusters of live oaks, tree plantings reinforced neighborhood identity without obstructing views. The intention of Ladera's sponsor had been to create a rural community, where people could "enjoy the advantages of country living, but without the high costs, isolation, and inconveniences we would face if we each tried to go it alone."[64] Their ideals validated Eckbo's arguments for the planning of cooperative farms during his tenure in the FSA.

Stein and Funk designed a dozen unit plans. The layouts ranged from compact square units complemented by paved surface and a small garden, to pin-wheel plans that extended their walls into the landscape to form green rooms, to bipolar plans in which the outdoor space penetrated the house to articulate the separation between sleeping and living areas. Overall, large expanses of glass increased the spatial perception of the houses from within and erased the division with the garden; Eckbo virtually mirrored the interior functions with complementary outdoor rooms—whether paved or carpeted with lawn—defined by hedges and screens. Ironically, the public play-

112
Ladera Housing Co-operative. Site plan. Palo Alto, 1946–49. Joseph Allen Stein, John Funk, architects; Nicholas Cirino, engineer; Eckbo, Royston and Williams, landscape architects.
Color pencil on diazo print.
[*Documents Collection*]

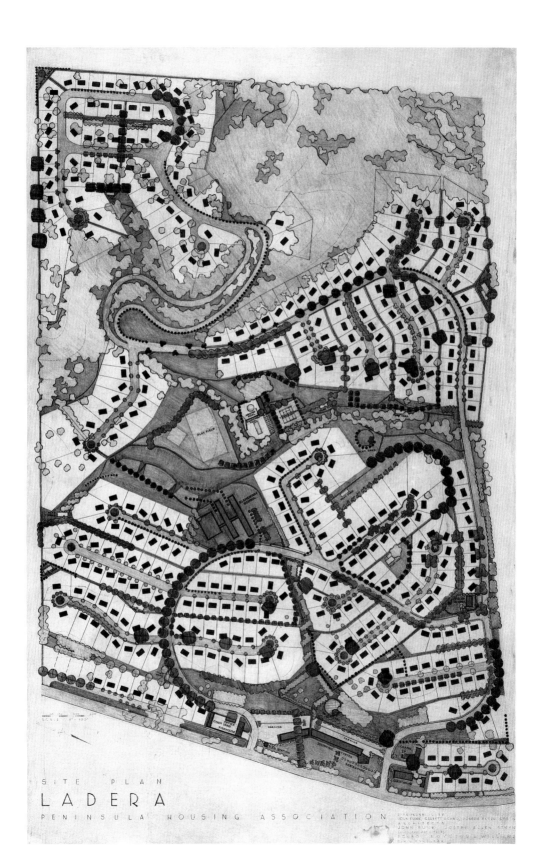

SITE PLAN
LADERA
PENINSULA HOUSING ASSOCIATION

113

**113**

Ladera Housing Co-opera-
tive. Playground for
children ages 5–11. Plan
and axonometric drawing.
Palo Alto, 1947.

[*from Garrett Eckbo*,
Landscape for Living]

**114**

Community Homes.
Site plan. Reseda, San
Fernando Valley, 1946–49.
Garrett Eckbo, landscape
architect; Gregory Ain
with Joseph Johnson and
Alfred Day, architects;
Simon Eisner, planner.
Ink on tracing paper.

[*Documents Collection*]

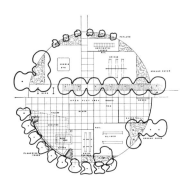

grounds were bounded by rectangular or circular perimeters like distant memories of the FSA parks constricted by the ideal geometries
of the site plan [figure 113].

Only a minimal part of the proposed overall layout and architecture
of Ladera was ever carried out, as the Federal Housing Authority
turned down the request for a construction loan — perhaps because
of the group's racial integration. By 1949, with 35 houses built using
individual financing — one house and lot at a time — the cooperative
association was dissolved and the site sold. The planning of Ladera
was then revised and partially redeveloped by Eichler Homes with
houses designed by architects Quincy Jones and Frederick Emmons.[65]

Before Ladera's construction — or rather its transformation — had
materialized, Eckbo moved to Los Angeles to nominally establish, in
1946, the southern branch of Eckbo, Royston and Williams. There, he
collaborated with Gregory Ain on several housing projects, of which
Community Homes in Reseda remains the most ambitious [figure
114]. In its social endeavor, democratic process, integration of architecture, private garden, and public landscape, its hierarchical favoring
of pedestrian circulation and greenery over infrastructure and automobile traffic it offered a postwar southern California suburban
equivalent to European, and in particular Swedish, cooperatives. As a
writer for *Arts and Architecture* stated, cooperatives "are successful
only when the need is real and close to the members' personal security. They atrophy or are vegetative when interest is passive and intellectual."[66] The project's architect was Gregory Ain, in collaboration
with Joseph Johnson and Alfred Day. The scheme grouped 280 single-family homes on 100 acres of flat land in the San Fernando Valley.
The overall plan — by Simon Eisner — formed a large L, articulated
by sixteen acres of open spaces that dissected each leg.

The two expansive "strip parks," and uniformly distributed "finger
parks," offered proximate recreational spaces for people of all ages
throughout the grid of houses and gardens [figure 115]. Recalling FSA
experiments in vegetal structure, Eckbo devised a master tree plan
with a "backbone" pattern of vertical formal accents — fan palm,
Canary Island pine, Lombardy poplar, incense cedar, Italian cypress,
and a large variety of eucalypts — as the ordering structure for a mix
of 79 types of trees. The rigor of this vegetal skeleton was offset by

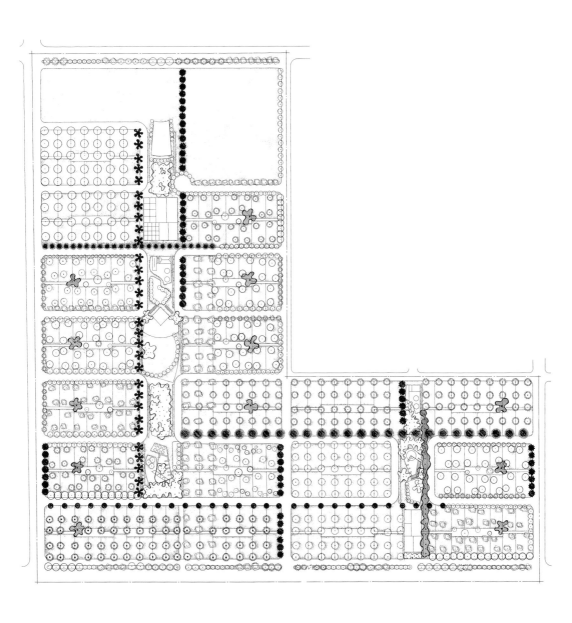

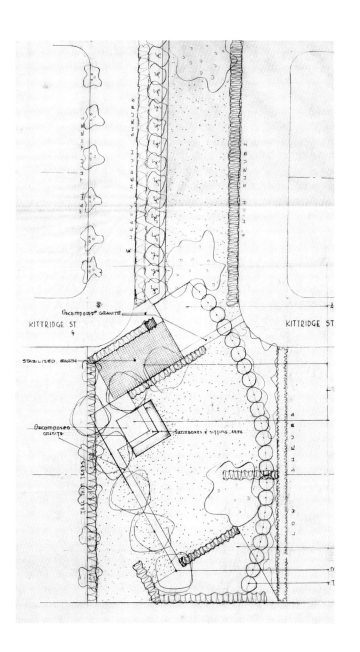

**115**
Community Homes,
Strip Park. Plan study.
Reseda, San Fernando
Valley, circa 1948.
Pencil on tracing paper.
[*Documents Collection*]

**116**
Community Homes.
Tree diagram. Reseda,
San Fernando Valley,
circa 1948.
Pencil on tracing paper.
High species included fan
palm and Canary Island
pine; medium species,
Italian stone pine, southern
magnolia, and camphor;
and low, purple-leaf plum
and photinia.
[*Documents Collection*]

**117**
Community Homes.
Tree diagram. Reseda,
San Fernando Valley,
circa 1948.
Pencil on tracing paper.
Here, Eckbo examines
spatial patterns in relation
to tree shape and texture.
[*Documents Collection*]

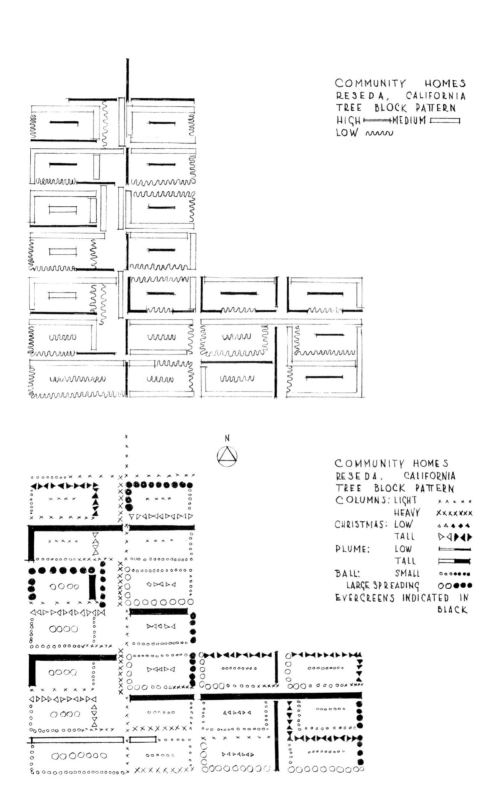

COMMUNITY HOMES
RESEDA, CALIFORNIA
TREE BLOCK PATTERN
HIGH ══════ MEDIUM ═════
LOW ∿∿∿∿

N

COMMUNITY HOMES
RESEDA, CALIFORNIA
TREE BLOCK PATTERN
COLUMNS: LIGHT     × × × × ×
         HEAVY     ×××××××
CHRISTMAS: LOW     ▵▵▴▴▵
           TALL    ▷◁▶◁▷
PLUME:   LOW       ▭═══▬
         TALL      ▬═══▭
BALL:    SMALL     ○○○○●●●
    LARGE SPREADING  ○○●●●
EVERGREENS INDICATED IN
              BLACK

the broader silhouettes of the "grove trees": London plane, Chinese elm, fruitless mulberry, cut-leaf silver maple, and weeping willow, and irregular plantings of shade trees, flowering trees, and fruit trees.[67] The tree plan was approved by the constituents via a thoroughly democratic process, Eckbo recalled, and like the landscape of the migrant camps, it drew from the "still rural character of much of the valley around it."[68] Tree patterns aimed to express neighborhood identity using spatial, structural, and textural qualities of the plantings. He alternated the heights of trees — low, high, and medium — and their shapes — columnar, "Christmas," plume, ball, and spreading. Transparency and the sense of enclosure varied within the architectural and planning matrix: a different order — that of vegetation — underlined yet subverted the uniform grid of houses.

Eckbo's diagrams included a significant amount of information, as they indicated height, density, shape, and whether the species was evergreen or deciduous [figures 116–17]. This graphically sophisticated encoding reveals upon study a wealth of spatial variations. Tall evergreen "plumes" essentially ran east-west, to provide shade against the southern exposure as well as a formal connection to the main recreation spine of the development — itself signaled by rows of palm trees. Eckbo suggested alternate scales within the grid of houses. By varying the height and opacity of vegetal enclosures he modified the planned order: blocks were either expanded — their unit boundaries minimized — or on the contrary, vegetation articulated the individuality of each cell within the suburban pattern.

Ain and Eckbo's integrated house and garden plans shared the clarity and simplicity of contemporary Ladera's spatial organization. As a juror, Ain had described the 1943 competition for "Designs for Postwar Living" — sponsored by *Arts and Architecture* — as a "Cooperative symposium." He saw the entries as reflecting what the "average citizen" required, indicating the "acceptance of a trend toward simplicity and directness… and the need to consider the relation of one dwelling to another. [The projects also affirmed] the need for 'livability' beyond the satisfaction of the purely mechanical functions of a house."[69] Such a stance would ultimately express his own approach to postwar housing, planning units in relation to one another and the community, with gardens that answered the interiors and a simplicity of execution that afforded maximum space with minimum means.

For Community Homes, Ain designed four typical house plans, whose variable configurations met the differing needs of their residents [figure 118]. Options ranged from compact two-bedroom, one-bathroom units, to slightly less compact three-bedroom, two-bathroom homes. When the dimensions of the kitchen precluded a breakfast nook, an opening between the cooking and dining-living areas allowed "the housewife to participate in social activities in the living room."[70] Sliding partitions permitted the conversion of two rooms into one. Overhangs, screens, and hedges extended the architecture into the garden.

Transparency — like the multiplication of interior rooms — made the outdoor space read as a paved mirror image of the living room, furnished with redwood rounds, specimen shrubs, and arbor [figure 119]. Similarly, Eckbo proposed alternative gardens according to needs and maintenance requirements, although none offered the vegetable plots of his earlier Flexible Co-op scheme. Possibilities ranged from a garden for the "active home farmer dirt gardener" to that for the "lazy one who just wants fun in the yard;" all fencing between lots balanced neighborliness with privacy.[71] To achieve a continuous landscape frontage along the street, he kept the vegetation open — with trees springing from planes of lawn or ground cover — limiting hedges or screens to the sheltering of the living spaces. In the backyard, on the other hand, Eckbo favored privacy and structured spaces, with arbors, flower beds, grape stakings, and "tall untrimmed hedges." This seclusion was not complete, however, as interruptions in hedges allowed a glimpse of, and passage to, the semi-public inner block "finger park." By separating cars from pedestrians, and interspersing greenbelt parks, pocket recreation spaces, and private gardens, Community Homes promised an alternative to more common suburban development [figure 120]. It would have been one of the most progressive experiments in communal home building, arguably unmatched in the United States since Radburn and Baldwin Hills Village.

During the postwar building boom, cooperative communities had become rather common endeavors—promoted in shelter magazines

**118**

Community Homes.
House and garden plan
(type "B"). Reseda, San
Fernando Valley, 1946–49.
Gregory Ain with Joseph
Johnson and Alfred Day,
architects; Garrett Eckbo,
landscape architect.
The gap in the backyard
hedge allows passage to
the "finger park."
[*from Garrett Eckbo,*
Landscape for Living]

**119**

Community Homes.
House and garden plan.
Reseda, San Fernando
Valley, 1946–49.
Gregory Ain with Joseph
Johnson and Alfred Day,
architects; Garrett Eckbo,
landscape architect.
[*from Garrett Eckbo,*
Landscape for Living]

"Our house is small but if
we handle it properly we
can extend our living space
right to the property lines."
[*from Richard Neutra,*
Mystery and Realities of
the Site, *in a review of the*
*book by Garrett Eckbo,*
*1951*]

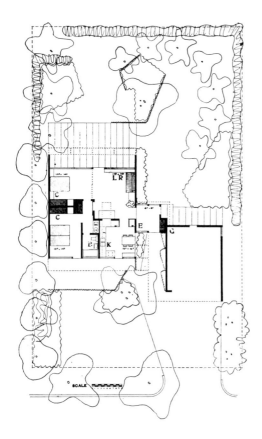

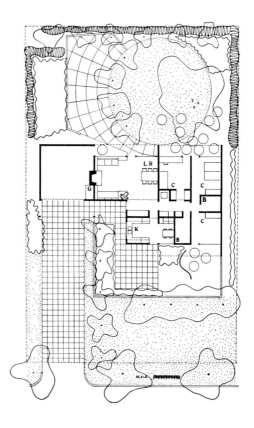

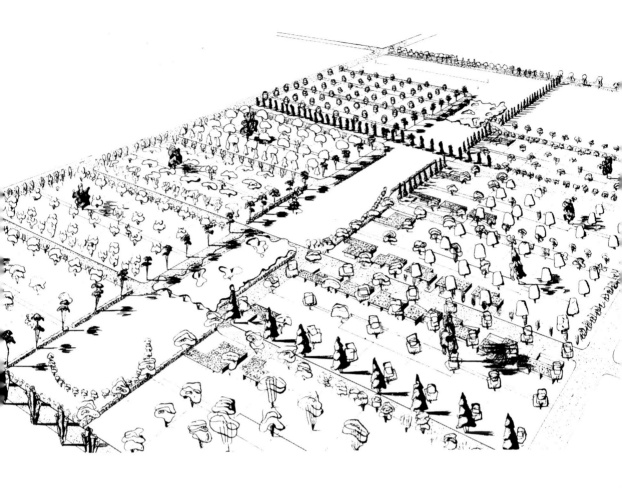

**120**

Community Homes.
Aerial perspective. Reseda,
San Fernando Valley,
1946–49. Garrett Eckbo,
landscape architect;
Gregory Ain with Joseph
Johnson and Alfred Day,
architects; Simon Eisner,
planner.

[*from Garrett Eckbo*,
Landscape for Living]

121

Park Planned Homes.
Site plan. Altadena,
1946-47.
Gregory Ain, architect.
[Courtesy Garrett Eckbo]

such as *House and Garden* — more typically resorting to convention-
al architectural expressions.[72] Those very tenets of defense housing
Eckbo had questioned seemed to direct Federal Housing Authority
programs, which subsidized home construction in terms of their sale
or resale value. Innovative design could thus prove a hindrance, as no
"theories or 'schools of thought'… should be allowed to interfere
with this clear expression of the law-making body."[73] Financing was
almost a formality for veterans without "too unconventional ideas
about architecture, nonsegregation or restrictive covenants," as
Vernon DeMars pointed out.[74]

Of course, Community Homes hardly fit the bill. The lengthy process
— three or four years spent organizing the group, purchasing the
land, meeting with various planning departments, and revising floor
plans — came to a grinding halt with the Federal Housing Authority's
decree that the inclusion of minorities jeopardized good business
practice.[75] DeMars noted:

> Co-operatives have traditionally insisted on nondiscrimination as
> to race, creed, and color, a rather academic consideration in
> England or Scandinavia, and one presenting no difficulty in run-
> ning a consumer's grocery store in the United States. Housing is
> something else again, and co-operatives should abandon not idea-
> lism but naïveté. Better housing is, in itself, a crusade — so is the
> co-operative way.[76]

The subscribers of Community Homes believed that better housing
should not abandon idealism: veterans of all races had fought in
the war. Bureaucracy prevailed, however, and the project was terminated through Regulation X, which prevented the Federal Housing
Authority from insuring loans for racially mixed developments.

## Community Landscapes

122

Park Planned Homes.
Altadena, 1947.
Gregory Ain, architect.
[Julius Shulman]

In 1946–47 Ain and Eckbo also designed Park Planned Homes, only a part
of which was realized [figure 121]. The subdivision was originally
planned to span four square blocks of Altadena, but of its projected
sixty units only twenty-eight were ever built — along a single street.
To increase economy, Ain resorted to semi-prefabrication. Savings
were ultimately minimal, however, with building crews demanding
higher wages for less labor. These practices confirmed Ain's prejudice

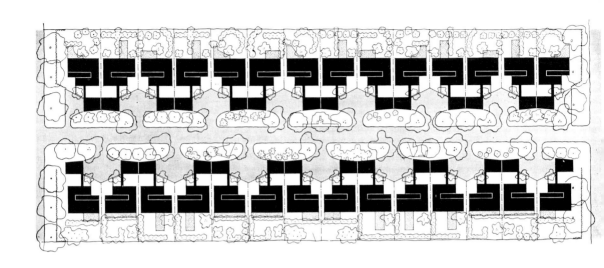

against standardization, which most contemporary architects seemed to consider an aim in itself, and an "incidental means to mass production of good dwellings."[77]

The 1,600 square-foot houses, oriented east-west, were placed on quarter-acre lots stepping down the incline of Highview Avenue [figure 122]. Of reasonable size, with three bedrooms and two baths, a patio-garden in the back and a play area/service yard in the front, large expanses of glazing and a clerestory for light and ventilation, the buildings offered openness and transparency without undermining privacy. The garages — paired and sharing a driveway — sheltered the service yard and children's play area from the street. Although both the site and floor plans show Eckbo's varied designs for individual gardens, the streetscape received his closest attention.

With the houses and garages set back from traffic, ninety-six-foot long planting strips provided a green transition between street and house. These islands of brilliantly colored flower beds were intended to combine with the varyingly painted street facades to relieve monotony. The planting schemes for Community Homes used trees to form linear spines or allées through the residential neighborhood and even to subvert its order. For a distinct identity, Eckbo usually keyed species to a block, a street, or at least a cluster of houses. The vegetation of Park Planned Homes was far more variegated within a smaller range [figure 123]. Here, he alternated heights and textures with each pair of garages and, coupled with the staggered driveways across the street, achieved a shifted allée of fragments. From the quincunxed planting strips sprang Lombardy poplar, olive, dwarf eucalyptus, and Mexican palm, to name only a few elements of the complex vegetal palette. Nearer the front door, the plantings became more regular — with Chinese pistachio marking the entrance to houses — culminating in the green frame of the hedges that outlined the rear gardens. With this variety of street trees, Eckbo established a play between street landscape and service yard, as private canopies emerged from behind enclosures and merged with the public landscape, making the latter part of the private realm while magnifying the streetscape of Highview Avenue.

Today, the image of Park Planned Homes is hardly that of an idyllic community, with collections of cars in various states of disrepair clut-

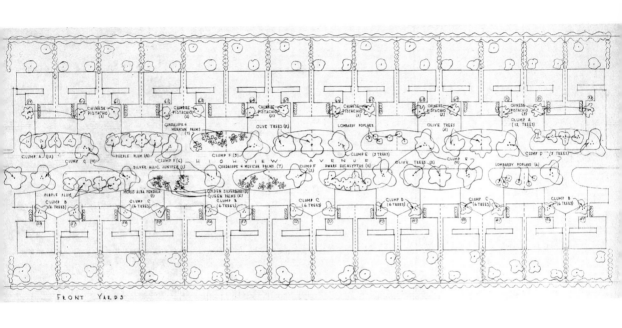

**123**
Park Planned Homes.
Planting plan
(27 February 1947).
Altadena.
Pencil on tracing paper.

[*Documents Collection*]

tering some driveways. The elegant balance of solid and voids has been distorted over the years, as additions were built and courtyards filled. A glance at the model of the original scheme affirms the idiosyncratic entente between Ain and Eckbo, whose interest in the social planning of housing communities outweighed that of designing luxurious individual houses and their gardens.

The two designers would renew their collaboration in Mar Vista, a planned development east of Venice [figure 124]. Completed in 1948 — if only partially, with only 52 of the intended 100 houses constructed — Mar Vista probably remains the most compelling evidence of a model joint venture among architect, landscape architect, and developer that would provide an alternative to the sterile productions of the "banker-builder-realtor trinity."[78] *Arts and Architecture* reported that to the Advanced Development Company, the project's developer, a house was not a mere commodity as it is for the typical builder — that is, an object to be bought and sold. Instead, it exemplified the "broader and more human definition of the word *commodity,*" that is to be convenient and provide amenity and accommodation.[79]

Modernique Homes (as the project was advertised) — of roughly 1,050 square feet on 75 x 104-foot lots — featured a basic unit type, with eight possible relations of house to garage and house to street [figure 125].[80] Intended to appeal to the average veteran, the house was situated on an average lot and intended to answer average needs. Modern planning fostered "full use of necessarily limited area; removal of living room from the main line of traffic through the house; direct connection of the living room with garden area away form the street; ease of maintenance, etc."[81] Sliding partitions provided flexibility within and increased a sense of openness and functionality. This description — equally applicable to the houses of Park Planned Homes and even Ladera — fit Ain's overall approach to low-cost housing, which he had already announced while judging the 1943 design competition for postwar living:

> A few plans, compact and well-studied, were eliminated early...
> as architectural clichés. They were well organized, had good inter-
> relation of rooms and gardens, and adaptability to restricted
> sites, and especially showed intelligent regard for the "Amenities
> of Living" (a cliché incidentally). They were reminiscent of some-

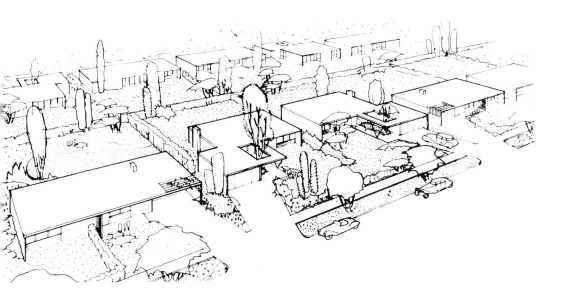

*thing that had already been done, but something that could well become a respected tradition. But it must not be forgotten that some clichés are so apt and forceful that they eventually became valuable additions to a vocabulary.*[82]

Similarly, Eckbo would refine his own clichés, or "valuable additions to a vocabulary" of landscape design and planning: neighborhood identity, relation of the individual to the group, manipulation of ground plane, spatial definition of overhead, and enclosure. He fully understood Ain's modest yet persevering attitude, later writing: "In all... Ain projects, the houses had a repetitive clarity with subtle variations. They challenged me to exploit variations in garden design for smaller spaces, and variations in street front treatment within overall unity" [figure 126].[83] Mar Vista was no exception, as Eckbo blurred once again the division between public and private domains, treating the buffer gardens as an expansion of the common green, and pulling the sidewalk away from traffic. He lined the streets with wide lawn strips and allées of magnolia on Meier, melaleuca on Moore, and ficus along one side of Beethoven. The character of each of these blocks varied greatly [figure 127]. With the allée of magnolia — a slow-growing species — the space is read as continuous from house to house, with the street causing a mere interruption to the texture of the predominantly linear green expanse. Dominating the houses on Moore Street, on the other hand, the vigorous melaleuca form a green nave resting on white trunks that divides the space as pedestrian-car-pedestrian [figure 128]. Finally, Beethoven Street stands as a case study of "before and after" or "if you don't do this, you'll get that" [see plate III]. Although ficus and magnolia are quite similar in their bearing and appropriateness as street trees, Meier and Beethoven streets lie worlds apart. Size, of course, is one issue, as the ficus firmly anchor the edge of the Modernique development. Ain's houses and Eckbo's plantings line only one side of Beethoven Street, with the other half displaying in full sun the hodgepodge of styles and yards that characterize most unplanned developments. Thus Mar Vista clearly demonstrated the superiority of intelligent planning as a vehicle for neighborhood amenity and identity.

The urban or suburban context dominated the equation among architecture, city, and landscape in the designs for Community Homes, Park Planned Homes, and Mar Vista. In contrast, landscape

**126**

Mar Vista Housing (Modernique Homes). Los Angeles, 1948. Gregory Ain, architect. Moore Street seen through an entrance atrium.

[*Julius Shulman*]

**127**

Mar Vista Housing (Modernique Homes). Los Angeles, 1948. Gregory Ain, architect. Meier Street, showing existing mature eucalyptus as well as newly planted magnolia.

[*Documents Collection*]

**128**

Mar Vista Housing (Modernique Homes). Los Angeles, 1948. Gregory Ain, architect. Moore Street today.

[*Marc Treib, 1996*]

**129**
Crestwood Hills
(Mutual Housing
Association).
Perspective sketch
of overall site.
Kenter Canyon,
Los Angeles, 1947–51.
Whitney Smith and
Quincy Jones, architects;
Edgardo Contini, engineer;
Garrett Eckbo, landscape
architect.
[*from Garrett Eckbo,
Landscape for Living*]

weighed the balance in the site planning of Crestwood Hills and Wonderland Park, as if on such hilly terrain, the human hand, or its design, was to bow against nature.

After the collapse of the Community Homes project, several of its members joined the Mutual Housing Association. This group grew to include 500 families by the time construction on Crestwood Hills began in 1949 [figure 129]. Eckbo collaborated with architects Whitney Smith and Quincy Jones, and engineer Edgardo Contini to produce the site plan. The topography of the 835-acre tract, situated in Kenter Canyon in western Los Angeles, ranged from flat to 30 percent slopes. The plan grouped houses along the two major ridges, with community facilities spread over the sycamore-covered valley floor. The aim of the design was to preserve views and limit grading along the ridges, maintaining a "natural profile." In contrast, the lower parts of the site — dissected by canyons — required massive grading, thereby resulting in a constructed landscape of stepped terraces. The house plans, sited on quarter-acre lots, offered variations in the basic structure of rigid wood frame with either concrete footings, piers, or steel beams dependent on terrain conditions.

**130**
Crestwood Hills
(Mutual Housing
Association).
Tree planting diagram.
Kenter Canyon,
Los Angeles, circa 1948.
The height and verticality
of species increase in
inverse proportion to the
elevation: from olive along
the ridges, to avocado,
cedar, and eucalyptus, and
to palm tree below.
[*from Garrett Eckbo,
Landscape for Living*]

Between the lines of the account Eckbo published in *Landscape for Living,* we can read the landscape architect's distance from the project's underlying philosophy. Crestwood Hills stood as the concrete manifestation of his ever-present argument that *natural* need not be the antithesis of *formal.* The site merged a "rough primeval" character with the "well-to-do residential neighborhood" below.[84] To Eckbo, a sophisticated vegetation plan provided the link between these two poles of human intervention; it also articulated topographic units while minimizing the perception of steep declivities [figure 130]. To achieve such a balance, low broad species would be planted atop the hills, moving toward taller columnar species as the elevation receded. Olive trees dominated the ridges, with some pockets of palms acting as buttresses; avocado spread along the intermediate elevation, followed by a mix of cypress, cedar, and pine, and further down, eucalyptus; poplar complemented the existing sycamores on the valley floor and completed the palette. As in Mar Vista and Community Homes, trees held the key to neighborhood identity. But in Crestwood Hills, they added a caption to the reading of the site's revised topography.

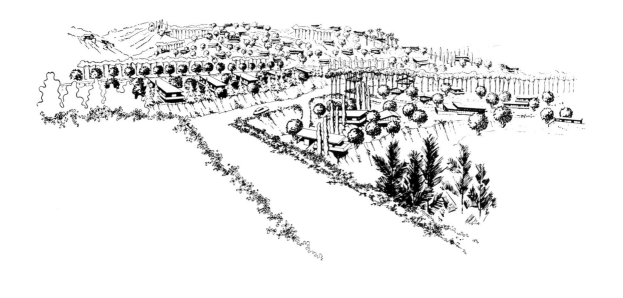

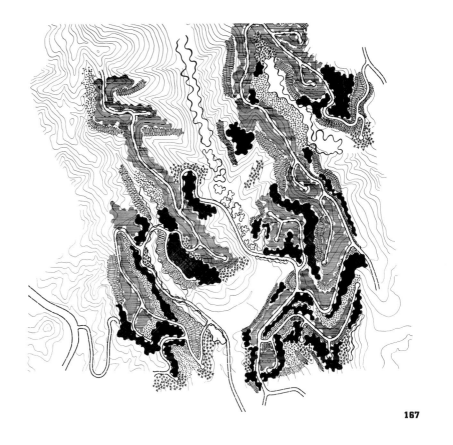

**131**

Crestwood Hills
(Mutual Housing
Association).
Typical garden plans.
Kenter Canyon,
Los Angeles, circa 1948.
[*from Garrett Eckbo,*
Landscape for Living]

The elaborate planting scheme was judged by Eckbo's clients as too variegated, too exotic, and thus "unnatural." Having always held that the role of design was "to improve the relationship between people and the landscape around them," the designer found the rejection of his thoughtful, recognizable plan a major disappointment.[85] In denouncing the favoring of "mechanical pepper-and-salt naturalism" over the "development of unprecedented spatial relations and humanized landscapes," he brought into focus the problematic and sempiternal quest for reproducing the image of nature, as opposed to shaping nature. The eighteenth-century legacy of the English "picturesque" haunted, and still haunts, the landscape architecture profession and the public's perception of what is "natural." As Eckbo pointed out, "it has been said that 'nature has no pattern,' therefore we should have none."[86] Thus, detractors argued, the visible imprint of human beings on Kenter Canyon needed to be minimized — as if to redeem the manipulation of five hundred thousand cubic yards of earth from its primeval state.

Eckbo also designed typical garden plans for Crestwood Hills [figure 131]. These he labeled also as "unnatural," given their "hav[ing] form;" they recalled the plays in boundaries and spatial manipulation initiated in Contempoville. The various configurations of hedges and tree enclosures defined functional areas within the garden and established a formal dialogue with the house. While partially outlining the edges of the site, these vegetal screens and anchors also dissolved the lot lines through fragmentation, as they distorted the boundaries' angled planes. One of the gardens was not only formal — with irregular checkerboards of lawn, gravel, rough deep grass — but it showed, once again, how vegetation was made to override geometry with its texture, color, and shape [figure 132]. He displayed orange persimmon against gravel; juxtaposed contrasting patterns of dark and light foliage; chose gray-green spindly melaleuca to form one allée and classical, dark-glossy-leaved magnolia for another; and considered floral and foliage color as well as fruit-bearing capability.[87]

**132**

Crestwood Hills
(Mutual Housing
Association).
Garden axonometric
drawing. Kenter Canyon,
Los Angeles, 1947.
[*from* The Californian]

Eckbo's tree master plan was never implemented, and the landscape of Crestwood Hills became "a collection of private designs."[88] He later compared this project with Community Homes in terms of client spirit. To him, the liberal and communitarian spirit of the Cartoonist and Screenwriters' Guild members not only provided a

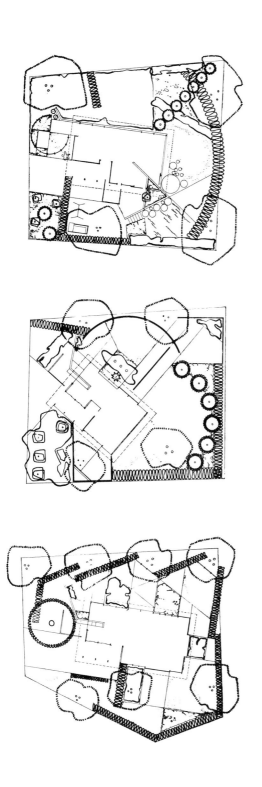

driving force for the design process of Community Homes but also guaranteed — or as it happens, prevented — its realization as a whole and as an expression of the social foundations of housing. The clientele of Mutual Housing, in contrast, came from a varied professional horizon, to the point that the member list was described in a publication as resembling a "vocational guidance bulletin."[89] Eckbo saw its common goal as the pursuit of economic advantages rather than the idealism of better housing communities through an expression of grassroots democracy.[90]

Approximately thirty-five other alumni of the Community Homes venture joined forces again to create Wonderland Park in Laurel Canyon [figure 133]. The tract, already subdivided — that is with its lines and infrastructure engraved in legal stone — would be developed for sixty-seven homes. For an economy of time and finances, the land was regraded to form a series of terraces; to counter the adverse conditions that compacted fill presented for gardening, brush was buried as soil amendment. Eckbo designed about half of the gardens for the Wonderland cooperative — including his own — and the arboreal master-plan for the valley [figure 134]. His overall scheme recalled that for Crestwood Hills; foresting the lower third of the site with tall, upright Canary Island pine, Italian cypress, and lemon gum [figure 135]. Ascending the hill, the vegetation gradually softened toward the broader canopies of camphor, olive, and oak. Again Eckbo mitigated the drastic rise in topography with an inverse progression in the scale of trees.

Late in the 1950s Eckbo reformed his own backyard at Wonderland Park into the ALCOA Forecast Garden [see figures 79–82; plates XIII, XIV]. He extended the modules of architecture into the garden, with roof overhangs, pergolas, and trellises of aluminum mesh, thus effacing the distinction between the interior and exterior rooms. Eckbo treated aluminum — an atypical material for garden structures, yet one with a very contemporary presence — as he would plants. As he had manipulated the space with lines of evergreen and deciduous trees, partitions of hedges, heterogeneous orchards, and zigzagging flower beds, he would exploit aluminum for enclosure, texture, shadow, light diffusion, transparency, and color. It was perhaps the very nature of aluminum that made the ALCOA Forecast Garden modern at the time of its creation and almost passé within very few years.

**133**
Wonderland Park.
Overall view.
Laurel Canyon,
Los Angeles, mid-1950s.
[Documents Collection]

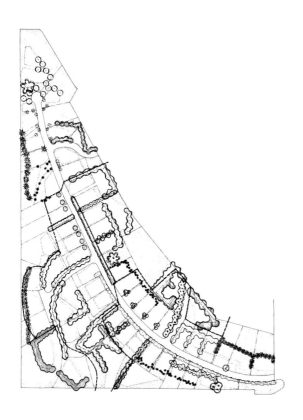

The landscape design for Wonderland Park thus illustrated the two sides of Garrett Eckbo: Eckbo, the collective persona, for whom the landscape was a testing ground for the group against — as well as for — the individual; and Eckbo, experimenting in pure sculptural forms — the garden as a haven, yet a vital unit of the neighborhood landscape.

In time, Wonderland Park also signaled the decline of the public's interest in social formation and better community housing. And if Eckbo's career as a garden designer continued to expand, his involvement with the greater landscape shifted toward ecological planning to the detriment of aesthetics and design. This was a turn he seemed to regret in the early 1980s as he pondered that "it remain[ed] to be seen whether the environmental movement [would] widen [the gap] or make it possible to reunite people and nature."[91] His message is still read today in the theoretical impact exerted by seminal texts such as *Landscape for Living*, the concrete remnants of plantings for the migrant camps in the Central Valley, or the structures of gardens. But perhaps his greatest contribution remains the understanding of people in the forming of rural and urban community landscapes. Insisting that "people are the focal points, the terminal features, the final vitality of any spatial enclosure we may create," he would deem necessary to consider what he termed "the open center" a principle of design.[92] As the so-called New Urbanists argue for suburban developments sufficiently dense to warrant the addition of shops, schools, and facilities for commerce or recreation within walking distance — all of them ingredients that Eckbo advocated as essential to a successful postwar community — we must ask why we turn to the distant past for solutions to the problems of today.[93] Instead, Garrett Eckbo would direct us to learn from society and the site — with faith in our ability to create our own landscapes appropriate to our own situation and times.

**134**
Wonderland Park.
Tree planting diagram.
Laurel Canyon,
Los Angeles,
circa 1950.
[*Documents Collection*]

**135**
Wonderland Park.
Street view.
Laurel Canyon,
Los Angeles,
mid-1950s.
[*Documents Collection*]

## Notes

1   Garrett Eckbo, "North vs. South," *Arts and Architecture* 1, no. 4 (1982): 40.

2   William Wurster, cited by Greg Hise, "Building Design as Social Art: The Public Architecture of William Wurster, 1935–1950," in *An Everyday Modernism: The Houses of William Wurster,* ed. Marc Treib (San Francisco: Museum of Modern Art; Berkeley: University of California Press, 1995), 145.

3   Christopher Tunnard, "Modern Gardens for Modern Houses," *Landscape Architecture* 32, no. 2 (January 1942): 60.

4   "A Model Block of Suburban Homes," thesis, Harvard University, 15 February 1938 (typescript, 1, courtesy Garrett Eckbo). Eckbo's intention to represent the "World of Day-after-Tomorrow" was a direct reference to the 1939 New York World's Fair "Tomorrowtown." An exhibition at New York's Museum of Modern Art had triggered a polemic on "Tomorrowtown's" lack of modernity, comparing it to the Stuttgart Werkbund of 1927. The captions of one exhibition panel read "New York World's Fair 1937 Designs… Today Looking toward Yesterday?" and "Stuttgart-Weissenhof Werkbund Exposition 1927… Yesterday Looking toward Tomorrow?" Eckbo included a reproduction of this panel in his scrapbook for Contempoville. See Henry-Russell Hitchcock's letter to the editors of *American Architect and Architecture* 151, no. 12 (December 1937): 16, 102.

5   See Detail Plans Lots 4-12-20, Contempoville, Los Angeles World Fair 1945 (Eckbo papers, College of Environmental Design Documents Collection, University of California at Berkeley [hereafter cited as Eckbo papers, Documents Collection]).

6   Garrett Eckbo, "Hypothetical Superblock Park, 1938," in *Landscape for Living,* 178.

7   Garrett Eckbo, "Outdoors and In: Gardens as Living Space." *Magazine of Art* 34, no. 8 (October 1941): 427.

8   "I was prepared to design the whole landscape, but I didn't have this other vision, or understanding. I was still undisciplined" (*Landscape Architecture: The Profession in California, 1935–1940, and Telesis.* Interviews conducted by Suzanne B. Riess, 1991 [Berkeley, Calif.: Regional Oral History Project, 1993], 28–29).

9   Gutheim also instigated the opportunity for Eckbo to work on the landscape plan for Norman Bel Geddes's General Motors Pavilion at the 1939 New York World's Fair (drawings dated November 1938). While in Washington, the landscape architect also collaborated with architects Kastner and Berla on the Federal Building at the 1939 San Francisco fair, designing its south court. Isometric drawing dated 16 October 1938 (Eckbo's own notebooks and Eckbo papers, Documents Collection). Dan Kiley replaced Eckbo in Washington, he recalls, allowing him to meet Louis I. Kahn and Eero Saarinen and helping launch his career (conversation with the authors, Berkeley, 22 April 1996).

10   See Garrett Eckbo, "Housing and Recreation." *Arts and Architecture* 63, no. 1 (January 1946): 34, and "Landscape Gardening II: Community Planting," *Architectural Forum* 86 (March 1946): 141.

11   From Marie De L. Welch, "The Nomad Harvesters," in *This Is Our Own* (New York: Macmillan, 1940), 56.

12   Frederic Delano, an advocate for Chicago's great advisory plan and later chairman of the committee for New York's comprehensive plan, fed his nephew's interest in planning. Frederic Delano directed the National Resources Committee, the first national planning agency, during the New Deal. See "The

Urban Pattern," in Works Progress Administration American Guide Series, *New York Panorama* (New York: Random House, 1938), 412–13; and Paul Conkin, *Tomorrow a New World: The New Deal Community Program* (1959; reprint, New York: Da Capo Press, 1976), 66.

13   Conkin, *Tomorrow a New World*, 38.

14   Franklin D. Roosevelt, cited in Conkin, *Tomorrow a New World*, 84.

15   "Such a romantic attitude is all too apparent among the American designers, who fail to see that the 'old swimming hole' needs lifeguards and pure water… or that the farm boy may be quite as interested in aviation or theatricals as his city cousin. On the other hand, there is the danger that — once recognizing these needs — the building or land-scape designer (because of his own urban background and experience) will uncritically apply *urban* design standards to a *rural* problem" (Garrett Eckbo, Daniel U. Kiley, and James C. Rose, "Landscape Design in the Rural Environment," *Architectural Record* [August 1939]: 68).

16   *Press-Herald*, Portland, Maine, 24 May 1936, cited in Conkin, *Tomorrow a New World*, 153.

17   See Carey McWilliams, *Factories in the Field* (Boston: Little, Brown, 1939), 294–95.

18   The State Relief Administration (SERA) first commissioned Paul Taylor to study the social conditions of the human river of agricultural laborers that flowed into California during the winter 1934–35. In 1935 Taylor invited photographer Dorothea Lange to join his team, thus marking the beginning of a long-lasting collaboration. Their report on the squalid state of life migrants had to endure is said to have influenced the federal govern-ment to enter this arena of emer-gency relief. See Sandra Phillips,

"Dorothea Lange: An American Photographer," in *Dorothea Lange: American Photographs*, ed. Therese Thau Heyman, Sandra Phillips, John Szarkowski (San Francisco: San Francisco Museum of Modern Art and Chronicle Books, 1994), 22.

19   McWilliams estimated the FSA attempted to provide assistance for 45,500 refugees in April 1938 (*Factories in the Field*, 308).

20   Talbot Hamlin, "Farm Security Administration: An Appraisal." *Pencil Points* (November 1941): 720.

21   Alfred Roth, "Co-operative Farm Community," in *Die Neue Architektur*, 61–70. Roth selected Richard Neutra's 1935 experimental school in Los Angeles as the other representative of "new" American architecture (105–14).

22   Garrett Eckbo, letter to the authors, 28 May 1996.

23   Hamlin, "Farm Security Administration," 710.

24   Garrett Eckbo, "Site Planning," *Architectural Forum* 76, no. 5 (May 1942): 263.

25   See Eckbo, "Outdoors and In," 422; Garrett Eckbo, "Space and People," *Architectural Record* (January 1950): 72.

26   "It is interesting to note how quickly *social integration* has followed *physical integration* in the new towns by TVA, FSA, and in the greenbelt towns of the former Resettlement Administration…. The recent west-ern projects of the Farm Security Administration — while of course designed for the landless migrants — clearly indicate the physical advantages of a concentration of housing facilities" (Eckbo, Kiley, and Rose, "Landscape Design in the Rural Environment," 71–72).

27   Albert Good, "Overnight and Organized Camp Facilities," in *Park and Recreation Structures* (Part III), 1.

28   For examples of National Park Service large organized camps see "Camp Layout" in *Park and Recreation Structures* (Part III), 114–19 (Eckbo, Kiley, and Rose, "Landscape Design in the Rural Environment," 74).

29   Eckbo, Kiley, and Rose, "Landscape Design in the Rural Environment," 74.

30   McWilliams, *Factories in the Field*, 324–25.

31   See Elizabeth Mock, *Built in USA since 1932* (New York: The Museum of Modern Art, 1945), 60–61; Hamlin, "Farm Security Administration," 712–14.

32   Hamlin, "Farm Security Administration," 713.

33   Mock, *Built in USA*, 61.

34   Vernon DeMars, "Social Planning for Western Agriculture," *Task*, no. 2 (1941): 9.

35   A phenomenon expressed within the process of hiring also, as McWilliams pointed out: "The established pattern has been some-what as follows: to bring in succes-sive minority groups; to exploit them until the advantages of exploitation have been exhausted; and then to expel them in favor of more readily exploitable material. In this manner the Chinese, the Japanese, the Filipinos, and the Mexicans have, as it were, been run through the hopper…. The latest army being recruited [was] from the stricken dust-bowl areas, from Oklahoma, Texas, Arkansas…. They came in without expense to the growers; they were excellent work-ers; they brought their families; they were so impoverished that they would work for whatever wage was offered" (*Factories in the Field*, 305–6).

36   "There was never a 'regional or traditional' expression specified.

Budgets and functional limits were strict. The few buildings were strictly functional. Most expressive or 'far out' were the two-story row house units which Burt [Cairns] and Vernon [DeMars] developed. They were like a touch of European modern in the western landscape" (Garrett Eckbo, letter to the authors, 28 May 1996).

37   See Weslaco file, Farm Security Administration (Eckbo papers, Documents Collection), and Eckbo, "Space and People," 72.

38   A principle Eckbo described as being inspired by Mies's architectural plans. See the caption to his garden for Mr. and Mrs. John Reid, Eckbo, "Space and People," 70.

39   Eckbo, "Site Planning," 266.

40   Hamlin, "Farm Security Administration," 711.

41   Garrett Eckbo, "Permanent Row Housing in Taft, California, 1941," in Landscape for Living, 206–7.

42   Eckbo, "Site Planning," 267.

43   Eckbo, "Outdoors and In," 425–26.

44   Eckbo, "Landscape Gardening II," 143.

45   Eckbo, "Site Planning," 266.

46   Garrett Eckbo, "Community Recreation Space in Ceres, Central Valley, California, 1940," in Landscape for Living, 179.

47   According to the FSA camps "constitution," residents served as the legislative and judiciary bodies, the manager acted as the executive, and all "worked together in an ideal microcosmic democracy" (Walter Stein, "A New Deal Experiment with Guided Democracy: The FSA Migrant Camps in California," Historical Papers [Toronto: Canadian Historical Association, 1970], 140).

48   Conkin, Tomorrow a New World, 186. An opinion also supported by McWilliams: "Although admittedly inadequate, the camps which have thus far been established are highly important institutions and foreshadow the appearance of a new rural social order in California" (Factories in the Field, 300).

49   See Stein, "A New Deal Experiment," 136.

50   Eckbo, Kiley, and Rose, "Landscape Design in the Rural Environment," 70.

51   See Cletus Daniel, Bitter Harvest: A History of California Farmworkers, 1870–1941 (1981; reprint, Berkeley: University of California Press, 1982), 270. Furthermore, to avoid political liability, agencies such as the WPA ruled as of 1935, that men could be released from work relief to report for work in the fields, regardless of the probable lower wage scale on the farm (Los Angeles Chamber of Commerce, Report of Special Labor Committee, 22 November 1935, cited in Daniel, Bitter Harvest, 272, 338 n. 18; McWilliams, Factories in the Field, 286–96).

52   "Before WW II camps residents were… Okies and Arkies. After they were black and chicano. (I went to see.)" (Garrett Eckbo, letter to the authors, 6 June 1996).

53   Daniel, Bitter Harvest, 284.

54   See Catherine Bauer, "Outline of War Housing," Task, no. 4 (1943): 5.

55   Eliel and Eero Saarinen, with Robert Swanson, designed 476 rental units for Center Line, Michigan, in 1941. See "5 House Types, One and Two Story, One to Three Bedrooms," Architectural Forum 75, no. 10 (October 1941): 229–31 and "Center Line, Michigan: 476 Permanent Units — Rental," Architectural Forum 76, no. 5 (May

1942): 281–84. In May 1942 Gropius and Breuer completed the 250 homes of Aluminum Terrace in New Kensington. See Isabel Bayley "New Kensington Saga," Task no. 5 (Spring 1944): 28–36. For Buckminster Fuller's "Dymaxion Deployment Unit" — a galvanized steel demountable tent — see "Building for Defense… 1,000 Houses a Day at $1,200 Each," Architectural Forum 74, no. 6 (June 1941): 425–29. On Wurster's defense housing at Vallejo and Sacramento, see Hise, "Building Design as Social Art," 138–63.

56   Catherine Bauer, transcript of Town Meeting of the Air, in "War-time Housing in Defense Area," Architect and Engineer (October 1942): 33.

57   See Lane Ryo Hirabayashi and James A. Hirabayashi, "Behind Barbed Wire," in The View from Within: Japanese American Art from the Internment Camps, 1942–45 (Los Angeles: Japanese American National Museum, UCLA Wight Art Gallery, UCLA Asian American Studies Center, 1992), 52.

58   Garrett Eckbo, "Trailer Housing Patterns in San Diego and Vallejo, California, 1942," in Landscape for Living, 204–5.

59   Eckbo, "Space and People," 75.

60   Eckbo, "Site Planning," 265.

61   Garrett Eckbo, "Farm Security Administration Projects," Arts and Architecture 1, no. 4 (1982): 42.

62   "Principles embodied in the drawings." See text accompanying plans for Flexible Co-op (Eckbo papers, Documents Collection).

63   Your Home in Ladera, Peninsula Housing Association brochure, 1947. Cited in Stephen White, Building in the Garden: The Architecture of Joseph Allen Stein in India and California (Oxford: Oxford University Press, 1993), 92.

64   *Your Home in Ladera*, 5, 12.

65   For the revised version of Ladera see "The Ladera Project," *Arts and Architecture* (July 1951).

66   "Mutual Housing Association: A Project for Five Hundred Families in Crestwood Hills," *Arts and Architecture* 65 (September 1948): 30.

67   Garrett Eckbo, General Tree Plan (Community Homes), June 1948 (Eckbo papers, Documents Collection).

68   Garrett Eckbo, "Co-operative Housing in the San Fernando Valley, Los Angeles, California, 1945–49," in *Landscape for Living*, 218–21.

69   See Gregory Ain's comments in "Designs for Postwar Living," *Arts and Architecture* 60 (August 1943): 27.

70   This description of Ain's Mar Vista designs equally applies to his planning for the houses of Community Homes. See "One Hundred Houses," 41.

71   Eckbo, *Landscape for Living*, 221.

72   See "If you are thinking of organizing a co-operative community…," in "Facts and Figures," *House and Garden*, February 1951, 110.

73   Eckbo, "Site Planning," 265.

74   Vernon DeMars, "Co-operative Housing—An Appraisal," *Progressive Architecture* 32, no. 2 (February 1951): 64.

75   Gregory Ain, cited by Esther McCoy in *The Second Generation*, 121.

76   DeMars, "Co-operative Housing," 77.

77   Gregory Ain, jury comment on "Designs for Postwar Living," 27. For Park Planned Homes, he instead sought to counter the rising costs of materials and construction with pre-

cut elements and jigs, such as those used to predrill holes in studs for wiring. He based the house plans on standard 12'×16' modules — a 12' module required only a single rafter size — and opted for longitudinal roof framing to eliminate beams over windows. Thus fenestration could extend fully to the ceiling.

78   Eckbo commended Richard Neutra for assigning blame for the lackluster urban and suburban developments to this "trinity." See Eckbo's review, "Richard Neutra on Building: Mystery and Realities of the Site," *Landscape Architecture* 42, no. 1 (October 1951): 41.

79   "One Hundred Houses," *Arts and Architecture* 65 (May 1948): 38, 40.

80   See *Arts and Architecture* 65 (September 1948): n.p.

81   "One Hundred Houses," 40.

82   Ain, "Designs for Postwar Living," 25.

83   Garrett Eckbo, "Cooperatives," *Arts and Architecture* 1, no. 4 (1982): 42.

84   Eckbo, "Co-operative Housing," 225.

85   "A Landscape Architect Creates New Dimensions in Landscaping with Aluminum," *Landscaping* (May 1960): 15.

86   Eckbo, "Co-operative Housing," 225.

87   For the typical garden plans, see Eckbo, "Co-operative Housing," 226. The above-mentioned garden is described by Virginia Scallon in "Now Is The Time and This Is The House… To Build," *The Californian*, July 1947, 49.

88   Eckbo, "Cooperatives," 42.

89   See "Mutual Housing Association," 32.

90   Conversation with the authors, Berkeley, 31 May 1996.

91   Eckbo, "North vs. South," 40.

92   Eckbo, "Space and People," 74.

93   See Herbert Muschamp, "Can New Urbanism Find Room for the Old?" *New York Times*, 2 June 1996, 27.

# AFTERWORD

## Garrett Eckbo

These have been good productive years (both aesthetically and socially), especially the twenty in southern California. Now, as I bow out, a new age is forming the next century. It will certainly be different. Architects and engineers seem heavily focused on increasingly rationalized construction that covers more and more of the Earth. It begins to justify various science fiction visions of a totally structured planet.

Parallel to this, the landscape architects and conservation people are focused on green open space within, around, and between cities, and the salvation of the natural landscape — whatever is left of it this year.

This is all well and good, but it misses the chief point of contention in the world landscape — the gap between structural and landscape visions. The former embodies the central outlook of the leading business/economic view of the world. It tolerates landscape visions but if they get in its way will not hesitate to ride over, and destroy, them. Its way embodies maximum profit for the chief protagonists.

The only way to save the world from the implications of this split attitude is to merge the two visions into a social/cultural/natural approach. That is the task for the coming century.

Garrett Eckbo in the
Aluminum Garden
during construction.
Summer, 1959
[*Julius Shulman*]

# A VIGNETTE

## Julius Shulman

A major contribution to my sixty years of photography, which has embraced a worldwide association with the giants, has been that of my extended friendship with Garrett Eckbo.

Beginning in the 1940s, when Garrett became a neighbor, we found a rewarding common ground of respect for the world of nature. And when the architect Raphael Soriano embarked upon the design of my home and studio, Garrett and I immediately engaged in a discussion on the ultimate development of the landscape program: in mutual respect we began an open-ended discussion of my family's two acres of natural hillside and how the landscape could help us keep our early associations with nature — beginning for me with my childhood in Connecticut. Now, forty-six years later, our house is literally engulfed in a jungle-like environment. The redwoods are 80 feet tall, with a girth of five feet! Without the equation of two individuals harmonizing on the same "beat" of tuned-in choices about design and planting, our intimate associations with scores of birds, animals, and resurgent native plants, we would have lost my longed-for goal of living as a "nature boy"!

I sincerely believe that all of the above grew from Garrett's ability to create a spirit of integrity as he pursued the project's programming and development. What a blessing!

12 June 1996

Shulman house.
Photograph taken about the time of occupancy, before planting had begun.
Laurel Canyon,
Los Angeles, 1951.
Raphael Soriano, architect;
Garrett Eckbo, landscape architect.
[*Julius Shulman*]

Shulman house.
Laurel Canyon,
Los Angeles, 1951.
circa 1980.
Raphael Soriano, architect;
Garrett Eckbo, landscape architect.
[*Julius Shulman*]

# BIOGRAPHICAL AND PROFESSIONAL CHRONOLOGY

Sammis garden. Berkeley,
1939. Sketch.

[*Courtesy Garret Eckbo*]

**1910**  28 November, born in
Cooperstown, New York, to
Theodora Munn and Axel Eckbo.

**1912**  Family leaves New York and moves
first to Chicago, then to Alameda,
California, where Eckbo spends his
childhood.

**1929**  Spends six months in Oslo with
paternal uncle, Eivind Eckbo, and
changes attitude toward study
and work.

**1932**  After working several years at
various jobs, attends Marin Junior
College.

**1933**  Enters the University of California at
Berkeley and majors in landscape
architecture.

**1934**  Designs Estate in the Manner of
Louis XIV as a studio project, his last
fascination with the formal garden.

**1935**  Graduates from Berkeley. Through
the auspices of Professor John
Gregg, Eckbo receives a position
at Armstrong Nurseries in Los
Angeles as a garden designer, where
he plans almost one hundred
gardens within a year.

**1936**  Submits competition for a scholarship
to Harvard University's Graduate
School of Design and wins first prize.

Enters Harvard University as graduate student in landscape architecture.

Bristles under the strictures of the
Beaux-Arts doctrine and, with classmates James Rose and Dan Kiley,
begins to explore science, architecture, and art as sources for a modern landscape design.

**1937** 19 September, marries Arline
Williams, sister of Berkeley
classmate and future partner
Edward Williams.

Continues graduate study, with
classes in architecture under
Walter Gropius — then department head — as well as in landscape design.

Designs Freeform Park and Small
Gardens in the City as student
projects.

Submits his master's thesis,
Contempoville, an examination of
the planned American suburb.

Shafter Unit. Pergola.
Tulare Basin, San Joaquin
Valley, circa 1940.
Farm Security Administration.
[*Documents Collection*]

**1938** Receives Master of Landscape
Architecture degree.

Works for six weeks in the office
of industrial designer Norman Bel
Geddes on the General Motors
Pavilion at the 1939 New York
World's Fair.

Invited by Frederick Gutheim,
works for the the United States
Housing Authority designing
prototypical recreation spaces and
courtyards for public housing.

Publishes "Small Gardens in the
City" in *Pencil Points* and "Sculpture
& Landscape Design" in *Magazine
of Art*.

ing camps for migrant agricultural
workers in California's Central
Valley, in Arizona, and in Texas.
Applies forefront modernist ideas
to these settlements for one of the
lowest strata of society.

With James Rose and Dan Kiley,
publishes three articles in
*Architectural Record* concerning
society, ecology, and landscape
architecture.

**1939** Returns to San Francisco.

Works for landscape architect
Thomas Church for about two
weeks.

Joins the western regional office of
the Farm Security Administration
[FSA], engaged primarily in design-

**1940** Joins with brother-in-law, Edward
Williams, to form Eckbo and
Williams while still at the FSA.
Executes some private
commissions.

**1942**  Because of the lingering effects of a 1939 automobile accident, Eckbo exempted from military service.

As the FSA turns its attention to defense housing, Eckbo designs about fifty projects during his tenure with the agency.

Works for several weeks in a Sausalito shipyard.

**1945**  Robert Royston is solicited as a partner for Eckbo, Royston and Williams while still serving in the Pacific theater.

The practice is soon recognized nationwide for innovative and carefully detailed work.

Eckbo begins to spend one week a month in Los Angeles, drumming up work, designing, and supervising projects.

**1946**  The Eckbos move to Los Angeles, first living in San Pedro, then various locations in the city; rents office space from architect Robert Alexander.

The Eckbo, Royston and Williams practice booms, undertaking hundreds of residential gardens, planned community developments, landscapes for churches, office and commercial structures, and educational facilities. Widely published in professional and trade journals.

Publishes articles in *Arts and Architecture* and other magazines.

Gold garden.
Los Angeles, early 1950s.
[*Documents Collection*]

**1948**  Francis Dean becomes partner in the firm; practice now includes college campus design in addition to schools, parks, and private gardens.

Eckbo begins teaching in the School of Architecture at the University of Southern California, continuing until 1956.

**1950**  Publishes first book, *Landscape for Living*.

**1952**  The Eckbos move to the Wonderland Park development in west Los Angeles; their house designed by Joseph van der Kar. Various schemes by Eckbo for the accompanying garden begin.

**1956** Approached by ALCOA Aluminum to design a "display": the Forecast Garden, using aluminum in its many forms and patterns as the principal material.

Publishes *The Art of Home Landscaping* (reissued as *Home Landscaping* in 1978).

**1958** Eckbo, Royston and Williams dissolved. Eckbo, Dean and Williams formed in the south; Royston, Hanamoto and Mayes in the north. Nature of the work begins to change, now engaged with more large-scale design and planning.

**1959** Completes ALCOA Forecast [Eckbo] Garden late in the year. Massive publicity campaign follows.

**1963** Returns to Berkeley to become chair of the Department of Landscape Architecture, University of California at Berkeley through 1969.

Designs the conversion of vehicular Fulton Street in Fresno to a pedestrian shopping mall. Continues work on the campus of the University of New Mexico in Albuquerque, which will extend over decades. Numerous other projects ranging from private gardens to major public commissions.

**1964** Eckbo, Dean, Austin and Williams (later known as EDAW) incorporated.

Publishes *Urban Landscape Design*.

**1969** Publishes *The Landscape We See*.

**1975** Receives the American Society of Landscape Architects' Medal of Honor.

**1978** Becomes Professor Emeritus at the University of California at Berkeley.

Publishes *Public Landscape: Six Essays on Government and Environmental Design in the San Francisco Bay Area*.

**1979** Leaves EDAW over differences in scope and type of work, and forms a series of smaller practices commencing with Garrett Eckbo and Associates. Major commissions include Shelby Farms, Memphis; Ojai General Plan; and environmental consultation with Saõ Paulo, Brazil.

**1983** Forms Eckbo Kay Associates with Kenneth Kay.

**1989** Reduces involvement in active practice, although continues to work on large-scale projects in California, Kuwait, and Japan.

**1990** Phases out remaining design work, devotes more time to theoretical study and publication.

**1996** Continues to write; book manuscript currently in press, *People in a Landscape*.

# BIBLIOGRAPHY

A.D.T. "Notes on Federal Activities Relating to Landscape Architecture." *Landscape Architecture* (October 1934): 41.

Albrecht, Donald, ed. *World War II and the American Dream*. Washington, D.C.: National Building Museum; Cambridge, Mass.: MIT Press, 1995.

"Apartments: Los Angeles, California." *Progressive Architecture* 33, no. 5 (May 1952): 82–83.

"Architect-Builder-Site-Home and Community, A. Quincy Jones and Frederick E. Emmons, Architects." In *Arts and Architecture: The Entenza Years*, ed. Barbara Goldstein, 154–55. Cambridge, Mass.: MIT Press, 1990. First published in *Arts and Architecture* (April 1952).

"Avenel Housing Associates: Los Angeles, California." *Progressive Architecture* 32, no. 2 (February 1951): 62–63.

Bannister, Turpin. "An Architect Looks at Landscape Architecture and Sees a Larger Demand for It than Ever Before." *Landscape Architecture* 39, no. 4 (July 1949): 164–66.

Barr, Alfred. *Cubism and Abstract Art*. New York: Museum of Modern Art, 1936.

Bauer, Catherine. "Description and Appraisal… Baldwin Hills Village." *Pencil Points* 25, no. 9 (September 1944): 46–60.

———. "Outline of War Housing." *Task*, no. 4 (1943): 5–8.

———. "War-time Housing in Defense Areas." *Architect and Engineer* 151, no. 1 (October 1942): 33–35.

Bayley, Isabel. "New Kensington Saga." *Task*, no. 5 (Spring 1944): 28–36.

Beneš, Mirka. "Inventing a Modern Sculpture Garden in 1939 at the Museum of Modern Art, New York." *Landscape Journal* (Spring 1994): 1–20.

Bressler, Eugene. "Chronological Summary, History of the Department of Landscape Architecture at Harvard University." Cambridge, Mass.: Department of Landscape Architecture, Harvard University, 1970.

Brown, Jane. *Gardens of a Golden Afternoon*. London: Penguin Books, 1982.

"Building for Defense… 1,000 Houses a Day at $1,200 Each." *Architectural Forum* 74, no. 6 (June 1941): 425–29.

Burn, Fritz. *Souvenir Pictorial Booklet of the Post-war House.*

Burnham, Heather, and Joel Davidson. "Chronology." In *World War II and the American Dream*, ed. Donald Albrecht, xxviii–xli. Washington, D.C.: National Building Museum; Cambridge, Mass.: MIT Press, 1995.

Byrd, Warren T., Jr., ed. *The Work of Garrett Eckbo: Landscapes for Living*. Proceedings of Annual Symposium on Landscape Architecture. Charlottesville: University of Virginia, School of Architecture, 1984.

"A California Plan for Indoor-Outdoor Privacy." *Architectural Record* 119, no. 5 (May 1956): 152–56.

Cammeerer, Arno. Introduction to *Park and Recreation Structures*, by Albert H. Good. Washington, D.C.: Department of the Interior, National Park Service, 1938.

"Center Line, Michigan: 476 Permanent Units — Rental." *Architectural Forum* 76, no. 5 (May 1942): 281–84.

Chase, John, ed. *A Sidewalk Companion to Santa Cruz Architecture*. Santa Cruz: Paper Visions Press, 1979.

Cheever, John. "The Swimmer." In *The Stories of John Cheever*. New York: Ballantine Books, 1982.

Church, Thomas. *Gardens Are for People*. New York: Reinhold, 1955.

"Come into the Garden: 300 Western Women Present the Garden Plan for Sunset House." *Sunset* (June 1939): 36–37.

"Community Church." *Arts and Architecture* 63 (May 1946): 36–37, 47.

"Concrete Panel House by Joseph Allen Stein." *Arts and Architecture* 66, no. 8 (August 1949): 20–21.

Conkin, Paul. *Tomorrow a New World: The New Deal Community Program*. Ithaca: Cornell University Press, 1959. Reprint, New York: Da Capo Press, 1976.

"Contemporary Jewelry by Margaret de Patta." *Arts and Architecture* 66, no. 9 (September 1949)

Daniel, Cletus. *Bitter Harvest: A History of California Farmworkers, 1870–1941*. Ithaca: Cornell University Press, 1981. Reprint, Berkeley: University of California Press, 1982.

DeMars, Vernon. "Bannockburn Cooperators, Inc.: Montgomery County, Maryland." *Progressive Architecture* 32, no. 2 (February 1951): 65–67.

———. "Co-operative Housing—An Appraisal." *Progressive Architecture* 32, no. 2 (February 1951): 60–61, 64, 77.

———. "Mutual Housing Association, Inc.: Los Angeles, California." *Progressive Architecture* 32, no. 2 (February 1951): 72–76.

———. "Peninsula Housing Association, Inc.: Palo Alto, California." *Progressive Architecture* 32, no. 2 (February 1951): 68–71.

———. "Social Planning for Western Agriculture." *Task*, no. 2 (1941): 4–9.

"De Patta." In *Arts and Architecture: The Entenza Years*, ed. Barbara Goldstein, 84, 244. Cambridge, Mass.: MIT Press, 1990. First published in *Arts and Architecture* (July 1947).

"Design for Postwar Living." *Arts and Architecture* 60 (December 1943): 22–25.

"Designing What Comes Naturally." *Architectural Record* 105, no. 6 (June 1949): 96–101.

"Designs for Postwar Living: Announcing the Winning Designs in the Architectural Competition Sponsored by California Arts and Architecture." *Arts and Architecture* 60 (August 1943): 22–37.

"Designs for Postwar Living Competition: 5 Entries Receiving Honorable Mention." *Arts and Architecture* 60 (September 1943): 19–31, 38.

Eckbo, Garrett. "Architecture and the Landscape." *Arts and Architecture* 81, no. 10 (October 1964): 22–23, 37–39.

———. *The Art of Home Landscaping*. New York: McGraw-Hill, 1956.

———. *Arts and Architecture [The Perception of Landscape]* 1, no. 4 (1982): 42.

———. "The Esthetics of Planting." In *Landscape Design*, San Francisco: San Francisco Museum of Art, 1948, pp. 16–18.

———. "Farm Security Administration Projects." *Arts and Architecture [The Perception of Landscape]* 1, no. 4 (1982): 41–42.

———. "Housing and Recreation." *Arts and Architecture* 63, no. 1 (January 1946): 34.

———. *An Interview with Garrett Eckbo*, January 1981. Conducted by Michael Laurie, ed. Karen Madsen. Watertown, Mass.: Hubbard Educational Trust, 1990.

———. *Landscape Architecture: The Profession in California, 1935–1940, and Telesis*. Interviews conducted by Suzanne B. Riess, 1991. Berkeley, Calif.: Regional Oral History Project, 1993.

———. "Landscape Design in the USA." *Architectural Review* 105, no. 625 (January 1949): 25–32.

———. *Landscape for Living*. New York: Duell, Sloan, and Pearce, 1950.

———. *The Landscape We See*. New York: McGraw-Hill, 1969.

———. "North vs. South." *Arts and Architecture [The Perception of Landscape]* 1, no. 4 (1982): 40.

———. "Outdoors and In: Gardens as Living Space." *Magazine of Art* 34, no. 8 (October 1941): 422–27.

———. "Pilgrim's Progress." In *Modern Landscape Architecture: A Critical Review*, ed. Marc Treib, 206–19. Cambridge, Mass.: MIT Press, 1993.

———. "Richard Neutra on Building: Mystery and Realities of the Site" (review). *Landscape Architecture* 42, no. 1 (October 1951): 41–42.

———. "Sculpture & Landscape Design." *Magazine of Art* 31, no. 4 (April 1938): 202–8, 250.

———. "Site Planning." *Architectural Forum* 76, no. 5 (May 1942): 263–67.

———. "Small Gardens in the City." *Pencil Points* (September 1937): 573–86.

———. "Space and People." *Architectural Record* 107, no. 1 (January 1950): 69–75.

———. "What Is Landscape Architecture?" *Arts and Architecture* 62 (October 1945): 40–41, 52.

———. "Wonderland Park." *Arts and Architecture [The Perception of Landscape]* 1, no. 4 (1982): 43–44.

Garrett Eckbo, ed. *Task*, no. 6 (Winter 1944–45), West Coast issue.

Eckbo, Garrett, Daniel U. Kiley, and James C. Rose. "Landscape Design in the Primeval Environment." *Architectural Record* 87, no. 2 (February 1940): 74–79.

———. "Landscape Design in the Rural Environment." *Architectural Record* 86, no. 8 (August 1939): 68–74.

———. "Landscape Design in the Urban Environment." *Architectural Record* 85, no. 5 (May 1939): 70–77.

*EDAW: The Integrated World. Process Architecture, #120* (September 1994).

"Edward A. Williams." *Landscape Architecture* 54, no. 2 (January 1964): 84.

"Farm Security Administration." *Architectural Forum* 71, no. 1 (January 1941): 2–16.

"Farm Security Administration: 72 Permanent Units — Rental, Taft, Calif." *Architectural Forum* 76, no. 5 (May 1942): 296–98.

"Farm Security Administration: 39 Prefabricated Duration Dormitories, Vallejo, Calif." *Architectural Forum* 76, no. 5 (May 1942): 334–37."

"5 House Types, One and Two Story, One to Three Bedrooms." *Architectural Forum* 75, no. 10 (October 1941): 229–31.

*FORECAST: LA.NDSCAPE*. Pittsburgh: Aluminum Company of America, n.d. (circa 1960).

"Future of the Profession." *Landscape Architecture* 53, no. 1 (October 1962): 25–26.

Gebhard, David, Harriette Von Breton, and Lauren Weiss. *The Architecture of Gregory Ain*. Santa Barbara: University of California, Santa Barbara Art Museum, 1980.

Goldsmith, Margaret Olthof. *Designs for Outdoor Living.* New York: George W. Stewart, 1941.

Goldstein, Barbara, ed. *Arts and Architecture: The Entenza Years.* Cambridge, Mass.: MIT Press, 1990.

Good, Albert H. *Park and Recreation Structures.* Washington, D.C.: Department of the Interior, National Park Service, 1938.

Gregory, Daniel. "Pasatiempo." In *A Sidewalk Companion to Santa Cruz Architecture,* ed. John Chase, 295–96. Santa Cruz: Paper Visions Press, 1979

Gropius, Walter. "Is There a Science of Design?" (1947). In *Scope of Total Architecture.* New York: Harper and Row, 1955.

———. "Scope of Total Architecture." In *Scope of Total Architecture.* New York: Harper and Row, 1955.

Gutheim, Frederick. "Greenbelt Revisited." *Magazine of Art* (January 1947): 16–20.

———. "Letter from Washington to a Planner in the Armed Forces." *Task,* no. 3 (October 1942): 9–11.

Halprin, Lawrence. "The Last 40 Years: A Personal Overview of Landscape Architecture in America." *Space Design,* Special Issue, *Gardens: Wonderland of Contrivance and Illusion* (1984): 5.

Hamlin, Talbot. "California: *Whys* and *Wherefores.*" *Pencil Points* 22, no. 5 (May 1941): 338–68.

———. "Farm Security Architecture." *Pencil Points* 22," no. 11 (November 1941): 709–20.

Heyman, Therese Thau, Sandra S. Phillips, and John Szarkowski. *Dorothea Lange: American Photographs.* San Francisco: San Francisco Museum of Modern Art and Chronicle Books, 1994.

Hise, Greg. "Building Design as Social Art: The Public Architecture of William Wurster, 1935–1950." In *An Everyday Modernism: The Houses of William Wurster,* ed. Marc Treib, 138–63. San Francisco: Museum of Modern Art; Berkeley: University of California Press, 1995.

———. "From Roadside Camps to Garden Homes: Housing and Community Planning for California's Migrant Work Force, 1935–1941." In *Gender, Class, and Shelter,* ed. Elizabeth Cromley and Carter Hudgins, 243–58. Perspectives in Vernacular Architecture 5. Knoxville: University of Tennessee Press, 1996.

"House for Dr. and Mrs. John Reid, Menlo Park, California." *Architectural Record* 103, no. 5 (May 1948): 122–25.

"House for Roger Kent." *Architectural Forum* 73, no. 12 (December 1940): 480–81.

"A House on a Hill for a Bachelor." *Arts and Architecture* 66, no. 5 (May 1949): 36–37.

Howard, Lee. "Five Hundred Building Bees." *Los Angeles Times Home Magazine,* 9 May 1948, 3–4.

Howett, Catherine. "Recreation Facilities in the United States." In *The Architecture of Western Gardens,* ed. Monique Mosser and Georges Teyssot, 510–11. Cambridge, Mass.: MIT Press, 1991.

Hubbard, Henry Vincent, and Theodora Kimball. *Introduction to the Study of Landscape Design.* New York: Macmillan, 1917.

Hudnut, Joseph. Preface to *The New Architecture and the Bauhaus,* by Walter Gropius. Trans. P. Morton Shand. London: Faber and Faber [circa 1936].

Huxley, Aldous. *After Many a Summer Dies the Swan.* 1939. Reprint, New York: Avon Books, 1952.

Imbert, Dorothée. "Of Gardens and Houses as Places to Live: Thomas Church and William Wurster." In *An Everyday Modernism: The Houses of William Wurster,* ed. Marc Treib, 114–37. San Francisco: Museum of Modern Art; Berkeley: University of California Press, 1995.

———. "A Model for Modernism: The Work and Influence of Pierre-Émile Legrain." In *Modern Landscape Architecture: A Critical Review,* ed. Marc Treib, 92–107. Cambridge, Mass.: MIT Press, 1993.

———. *The Modernist Garden in France.* New Haven: Yale University Press, 1993.

Jackson, Helen Hunt. *Ramona.* New York: Grosset and Dunlap, 1884.

Jackson, John Brinckerhoff. "The Word Itself." In *Defining the Vernacular Landscape.* New Haven: Yale University Press, 1984.

Kandinsky, Wassily. *On the Spiritual in Art.* Trans. M.T.H. Sadler. 1914. Reprint, New York: Dover Publications, 1977.

Kennedy, Robert W. "Garden Variety" (review of *Landscape for Living,* by Garrett Eckbo). *Architectural Record* 108, no. 8 (August 1950): 28.

Kirker, Harold. *California's Architectural Frontier: Style and Tradition in the Nineteenth Century.* Santa Barbara: Peregrine Smith, 1973.

Klee, Paul. *Pedagogical Sketchbook.* 1925. Trans. Sibyl Moholy-Nagy. New York: Frederick Praeger, 1953.

"The Ladera Project: A. Quincy Jones, Frederick Emmons, Architects." *Arts and Architecture* 68 (July 1951): 27–31.

*Landscape Design.* Exhibition catalog. San Francisco: San Francisco Museum of Art, 1948.

"Landscape Gardening II: Community Planting." *Architectural Forum* 84, no. 5 (March 1946): 141–44.

*Landscaping for Modern Living.* Sunset magazine editors. Menlo Park, California: Lane Publishing, 1956.

Lao Tzu. *Tao Te Ching.* Trans. D. C. Lau. Baltimore: Penguin Books, 1963.

Laurie, Michael. "The California Garden: No Place to Go?" *Landscape Architecture* 56, no. 1 (October 1965): 23–27.

———. "From Garden Design to Regional Plan: The California Influence on Contemporary Landscape Architecture." *Landscape Architecture* 56, no. 4 (July 1966): 292–98.

———. "The Modern California Garden." *Pacific Horticulture* 54, no. 2 (Summer 1993): 22–25.

Laurie, Michael, and David Streatfield. *75 Years of Landscape Architecture at Berkeley: An Informal History. Part I: The First 50 Years.* Berkeley: Department of Landscape Architecture, University of California at Berkeley, 1988.

"Livability on a Small, Hilly Lot." *Architectural Record* 109, no. 6 (June 1951): 168–71.

"Low Cost Contemporary House by A. Quincy Jones, Architect." *Arts and Architecture* 66, no. 9 (September 1949): 35–37.

McCoy, Esther. "Garrett Eckbo: The Early Years." *Arts and Architecture [The Perception of Landscape]* 1, no. 4 (1982): 39–40.

———. *Modern California Houses: Case Study Houses 1945–1962.* New York: Reinhold, 1962.

———. *The Second Generation.* Salt Lake City: Gibbs Smith, 1984.

McHarg, Ian. *Design with Nature.* Garden City, N.Y.: Doubleday, 1966.

McWilliams, Carey. *Factories in the Field: The Story of Migratory Farm Labor in California.* Boston: Little, Brown, 1939.

Meyer, Elizabeth K. "The Modern Framework." *Landscape Architecture* 73, no. 2 (March–April 1983): 50–52.

Miró, Joan. *Je travaille comme un jardinier.* Paris: Société Internationale d'Art du XX° Siècle, 1964.

Mock, Elizabeth, ed. *Built in USA since 1932.* New York: Museum of Modern Art, 1945.

Moss, Stacey. *The Howards: First Family of Bay Area Modernism.* Oakland: Oakland Museum, 1988.

"Mutual Housing Association: A Project for Five Hundred Families in Crestwood Hills." *Arts and Architecture* 65 (September 1948): 30–43.

"Mutual Housings Pilot House." *Arts and Architecture* 66, no. 3 (March 1949): 42–43.

Neckar, Lance. "Christopher Tunnard: The Garden in the Modern Landscape." In *Modern Landscape Architecture: A Critical Review,* ed. Marc Treib, 145–58. Cambridge, Mass.: MIT Press, 1993.

———. "Strident Modernism / Ambivalent Reconsiderations: Christopher Tunnard's *Gardens in the Modern Landscape.*" *Journal of Garden History* 10 (1990): 237–46.

"The New House-to-Site Transition." *Progressive Architecture* 37, no. 6 (June 1956): 106–13.

O'Malley, Therese, and Marc Treib, eds. *Regional Garden Design in the United States.* Washington, D.C.: Dumbarton Oaks, 1995.

"One Hundred Houses." *Arts and Architecture* 65, no. 5 (May 1948): 38–41.

"One of a Hundred — Gregory Ain, Architect, Joseph Johnson, Alfred Day, Collaborating." *Arts and Architecture* 66, no. 9 (September 1949): 40–41.

"Park Planned Homes, Altadena, California." *Progressive Architecture* 28, no. 7 (July 1947): 66–69.

Partridge, Loren W. *John Galen Howard and the Berkeley Campus: Beaux-Arts Architecture in the "Athens of the West."* Berkeley: Berkeley Architectural Heritage Association, 1978.

"Pasadena Design Solves Uneven Site Problem." *Architectural Record* 119, no. 5 (May 1956): 180–83.

"Peninsula Cooperative." *Arts and Architecture* 65 (January 1948): 37–40.

Pratt, Richard. "Home for the Veteran." *Ladies Home Journal,* May 1945, 146–47.

"Productive Garden Homes." *Pencil Points* 20, no. 5 (May 1939): 307–14.

"A Professional Adventure in Use of Outdoor Space." *Architect and Engineer* 166, no. 3 (September 1946): 11–23.

Rainey, Reuben. " 'Organic Form in the Humanized Landscape:' Garrett Eckbo's *Landscape for Living.*" In *Modern Landscape Architecture: A Critical Review,* ed. Marc Treib, 180–205. Cambridge, Mass.: MIT Press, 1993.

Reed, Peter. "Enlisting Modernism." In *World War II and the American Dream,* ed. Donald Albrecht, 2–41. Washington, D.C.: National Building Museum; Cambridge, Mass.: MIT Press, 1995.

"Residential Development." *Architectural Forum* 83, no. 11 (November 1945): 136–39.

Rose, James C. "Freedom in the Garden: A Contemporary Approach in Landscape Design." *Pencil Points* 19, no. 10 (October 1938): 639–43.

———. "Gardens." *California Arts and Architecture* 57, no. 5 (May 1940): 20.

———. "Modular Gardens." *Progressive Architecture* 28, no. 9 (September 1947): 76–80.

———. "Why Not Try Science?" *Pencil Points* 20, no. 12 (December 1939): 777–79.

Roth, Alfred. *Die Neue Architektur 1930–1940.* 1939. Reprint, Zürich: Verlag für Architektur Artemis, 1975.

Royston, Robert. "A Brief History." *Landscape Australia* (Summer 1986): 34–36.

———. "Point of View / Robert Royston." *Landscape Architecture* 76, no. 6 (November–December 1986): 66–67, 116.

Scallon, Virginia. "Now Is The Time and This Is The House ... To Build." *The Californian*, July 1947, 48–51.

"The Shape of Shade to Come." *House and Garden*, April 1960, 155–57.

"Show Place Like Home." *Architectural Record* 99, no. 4 (April 1946): 90–99.

Simo, Melanie. "The Education of a Modern Landscape Designer." *Pacific Horticulture* 49, no. 2 (Summer 1988): 19–30.

"Small House." *Arts and Architecture* 64 (March 1947): 30.

"A Small House of 485 Square Feet by Albert Henry Hill." *Arts and Architecture* 66, no. 6 (June 1949): 30–31.

"Small Redwood Country House." *Arts and Architecture* 59 (February 1942): 28–29.

Smith, Elizabeth A.T., curator. *Blueprints for Modern Living: History and Legacy of the Case Study Houses*. Ed. Howard Singerman. Los Angeles: Museum of Contemporary Art; Cambridge, Mass.: MIT Press, 1989.

Soby, James Thrall. *Joan Miró*. New York: Museum of Modern Art, 1959.

"Speech Arts Building." *Progressive Architecture* 36, no. 12 (December 1955): 104–9.

Steele, Fletcher. "New Pioneering in Garden Design." *Landscape Architecture* 20, no. 3 (April 1930): 158–77.

Stein, Walter. "A New Deal Experiment with Guided Democracy: The FSA Migrant Camps in California." *Historical Papers* (Toronto : Canadian Historical Association, 1970): 132–46.

Steinbeck, John. *The Grapes of Wrath*, 1939. Reprint, New York: Penguin Books, 1967.

Steiner, Michael C. "Regionalism in the Great Depression." *The Geographical Review* 73, no. 4 (October 1983): 430–46.

"A Step-back Plan on a Hillside Site Gives Privacy to Ten Los Angeles Families." *House and Garden*, February 1951, 50–51, 110.

Streatfield, David. *California Gardens: Creating a New Eden*. New York: Abbeville Press, 1994.

"Subdivision by Gregory Ain, A.I.A., Architect for Park Planned Homes." *Arts and Architecture* 62 (November 1945): 32–35.

"Sunset and 300 Western Women Build a Home." *Sunset*, March 1939, 20–21.

"Sunset House Multiplanned by 300 Western Women." *Sunset*, May 1939, 34–35.

"Sunset House: Revised to Meet the Budget." *Sunset*, October 1939, 27.

Thompson, J. William. "Standard-Bearer of Modernism." *Landscape Architecture* 80, no. 2 (February 1990): 88–95.

"300 Western Women Start Planning Sunset House." *Sunset*, April 1939, 48–49.

Treib, Marc. "Aspects of Regionality and the Modern(ist) Garden in California." In *Regional Garden Design in the United States*, ed. Therese O'Malley and Marc Treib, 5–42. Washington, D.C.: Dumbarton Oaks, 1995.

———. "Axioms for a Modern Landscape Architecture." In *Modern Landscape Architecture: A Critical Review*, ed. Marc Treib, 36–67. Cambridge, Mass.: MIT Press, 1993.

———. "A Feeling for Function." In *An Everyday Modernism: The Houses of William Wurster*, ed. Marc Treib, 12–83. San Francisco: Museum of Modern Art; Berkeley: University of California Press, 1995.

Marc Treib, ed. *An Everyday Modernism: The Houses of William Wurster*. San Francisco: Museum of Modern Art; Berkeley: University of California Press, 1995.

———. *Modern Landscape Architecture: A Critical Review*. Cambridge, Mass.: MIT Press, 1993.

Tsujimoto, Karen. *Dorothea Lange: Archives of an Artist*. Oakland: Oakland Museum of California, 1995.

Tunnard, Christopher. "Art and Landscape Design: A Talk Given at the Ann Arbor Conference on Aesthetics." *Landscape Architecture* 39, no. 3 (April 1949): 104–10.

———. *Gardens in the Modern Landscape*. 2d ed. London: Architectural Press, 1948.

———. "Modern Gardens for Modern Houses: Reflections on Current Trends in Landscape Design." *Landscape Architecture* 32 , no. 2 (January 1942): 57–64.

"Vacation Houses." *Architectural Forum* 95, no. 2 (August 1957): 156–61.

Walker, Peter, and Melanie Simo. *Invisible Gardens*. Cambridge, Mass.: MIT Press, 1994.

Welch, Marie de L. *This Is Our Own*. New York: Macmillan, 1940.

"West Los Angeles, California." *Progressive Architecture* 36, no. 5 (May 1955): 116–21.

White, Stephen. *Building in the Garden: The Architecture of Joseph Allen Stein in India and California*. Oxford: Oxford University Press, 1993.

# INDEX